AMERICAN MUSLIMS

MUSLIMS

Bridging Faith and Freedom

First Edition
(1423AH/2002AC)

© Copyright 1423AH/2002AC
amana publications
10710 Tucker Street
Beltsville, Maryland 20705-2223 USA
Tel: (301) 595-5777 / Fax: (301) 595-5888
E-mail: amana@igprinting.com
Website: www.amana-publications.com

Library of Congress Cataloging-in-Publications Data

Khan, Muqtedar.
  American Muslims : bridging faith and freedom / Muqtedar Khan.
      p. cm.
  ISBN 1-59008-012-2
  1. Muslims--United States. 2. Islam and state--United States. 3.
Islam and politics--United States. 4. Freedom of religion--United
States. 5. United States--Ethnic relations. 6. United States--Politics
and government. I. Title.
BP67.U6 K47 2002
305.6'971073--dc21

                                        2002010230

Printed in the United States of America by
International Graphics
10710 Tucker Street
Beltsville, Maryland 20705-2223 USA
Tel: (301) 595-5999 Fax: (301) 595-5888
Website: igprinting.com
E-mail: ig@igprinting.com

AMERICAN MUSLIMS

Bridging Faith and Freedom

M. A. Muqtedar Khan, Ph.D.
Director of International Studies
Adrian College, Adrian, MI, USA

Foreword by Akbar S. Ahmed

amana publications

For my Father,
Mohommed Abdul Hafeez Khan; 1939-2001.

It was through the example of his life that I learnt
the true meaning of *Jihad* (Struggle) and *Ihsan* (Excellence).
He taught me that the true relation between father and son
is like the one between a teacher and his disciple.

*But We have indeed made
the Qur'an easy to understand and remember:
then is there any that will receive admonition?*

– Qur'an 54: 17

TABLE OF CONTENTS

Foreword

The Nineteen hijackers on September 11, 2001 challenged the world by their violent act. But they also challenged their own faith of Islam. In the light of the tragic deaths of thousands of innocent people many questions about Islam were thrown up: Why do they hate us? Is Islam compatible with democracy? Does the *Qur'an* preach violence?

These questions were being asked by everyone: from the President of the United States to the proverbial man in the street. Muslims had to provide the answers. Fortunately, for the Muslim community in America there were many sane and learned voices. One of the most prominent was Dr. Muqtedar Khan.

Dr. Muqtedar Khan emerged after September 11 as a leading spokesman of the Muslim community. He appeared to be indefatigable and ubiquitous. He was in the print media and in the visual one; he was on the lecture circuit; and he was on the Internet.

In a sense, the last decade had prepared Dr. Muqtedar Khan for his role. His academic training at Georgetown — from where he received a Ph.D. in international relations, Islamic political thought, and philosophy — and his earlier training as an executive in India had prepared him well. He had already been grappling with questions about the role of democracy and women in Islam, the directions of politics and questions of leadership.

Dr. Khan had arrived in America from India to find a dramatically different world and yet in some senses familiar to him. He was after all a member of a minority community in India, confronting some of the same questions about Muslims. Growing up in Hyderabad, in a comfortable middle class family, which placed an emphasis on education, he became aware of some of the problems facing the Muslim community in America even before September 11.

The Muslims in America are a powerful presence with about 7 million in number. They are divided into three distinct but sometimes overlapping and interconnected communities with about the same numbers. Firstly, the Afro-Americans who brought Islam to America from Africa centuries ago; secondly, the Middle East communities who started to come even before the Second World War but in large numbers after the end of the War; and thirdly, South Asians who came towards the end of the 20th century.

Muslim leadership tends to be localized and usually based in its own community. There are some but not many examples of Muslim leaders who transcend the communities into an overarching Muslim identity. As leadership tends to be community based there is little room for the role of the public intellectual. September 11 changed all that.

The other kind of leadership in the Muslim community is mosque-based. Those who run and organize mosques tend to reflect the community generally: a mosque organized by South Asians will often have an imam from South Asia. Here, too, there is little scope in the traditional structure for the role of a public intellectual.

Dr. Muqtedar Khan stepped felicitously into the role of the public intellectual explaining Islam in the media after September 11. His personal journey of the discovery of Islam in his new country and the desire of his new country to learn of his faith met. Dr. Khan employed his technological and intellectual capabilities to begin the process of asking and raising questions.

Not all Muslims are pleased with what Dr. Khan writes. Some find his opinions and analysis difficult to swallow. But what cannot be denied is that Dr. Khan makes the community take notice of his ideas. And he is writing consciously as a committed Muslim who believes that Islam is compatible with reason, democracy and universal toler-ance. He believes that the more compassionate understanding of the world, the more Islamic the world is. That is why there is a need for *Ijtihad* – or innovative thinking in Islam. Indeed, he calls his website www.ijtihad.org.

I am delighted to be writing the foreword to Muqtedar Khan's book on Islam in America. He has raised many important questions that need answers; he has pointed to political and social directions for the community; he has argued for the compassionate interpretation of faith; he has, at the same time, courageously pointed out the needs of the community that the majority population must address; and final-ly, he has conveyed a message of tolerance and understanding. To my mind, Dr. Muqtedar Khan has lived up to the challenging role of the public intellectual in a time of crisis.

– Professor Akbar S. Ahmed
Ibn Khaldun Chair of Islamic Studies and
Professor of International Relations
School of International Service
American University, Washington, DC 20016

Preface

In the name of Allah, Most Merciful, Most Benevolent.

A book is a journey that in the least accomplishes two things. It pays homage to the experiences, the people and the ideas that have shaped the author and also clarifies issues that agitate one's intellectual curiosity. In that sense a book is essentially a journey of self-discovery. If anything, in this book I have found the meaning of my life, to speak with a voice of moderation and justice. I have also discovered, if only for myself, what is involved in living life as a believing Muslim in an age that is plagued by a crisis of legitimacy.

When living in a society that has abandoned the quest for truth in favor of conventions, that has replaced traditional wisdom with contemporary public opinion, intellectual life inevitably becomes a search for meaning and substance and above all connection. In my quest to understand the Qur'anic mandate to Muslims to become a community of moderation (*Qur'an* 3: 104), I have found that making the right connections is the key to discovering meaning and purpose. Therefore in this book I have tried to connect with the *Qur'an* (Text) with one hand and the world (context) with the other. The tensions in this book, the inconsistencies, the struggle for order, for comprehension and for simplicity despite the unfathomable complexity of reality and of texts, basically manifest my personal struggle to come to terms with the demands of late modern America and the injunctions of Islam.

I have worked with two basic assumptions. First, that *Qur'an* is indeed the revealed word of God and second that reason is the receptacle of revelation. I assume that the divine message is *understandable* by the human subject and proceed to seek an understanding from the standpoint of a Muslim living in America. I am convinced that while there is an absolute Truth with a capital T, it remains transcendent. We can only grab contextual understandings of the Truth and these time and space bound truths become the normative principles of our age and place.

This book therefore is a struggle to articulate the normative principles that can guide Muslims who live *now* and *in* America.

This book is not the work of a jurist or a historian or even a social scientist. I would like it to be read as the work of a contemporary Islamic philosopher, whose intellectual lenses are framed within the Islamic tradition and are focused on the here and the now. Nothing in terms of topics is beyond the scope of the book. But the scope of the book itself is limited in the extent to which it explores specific topics. It is in essence a collection of thoughts, a necklace of ideas, seeking to re-understand Islamic principles and comprehend the conditions of Muslim existence within the confines of this re-understanding of Islam. The book seeks to provoke thought, open new avenues of thinking and challenges Muslims to critically re-examine some of their fossilized interpretations of Islam.

In this journey I have accumulated a large amount of material, intellectual and spiritual debt. I wish to thank everyone who taught me, argued with me, supported me and criticized me. I have learned a lot from all those intellectual encounters.

I wish to make special mention of two women who are the two pillars of my life. Without their love and support I would not be able to function as an adequate human being. They are my mother, Afzalunnisa and my wife Reshma. I am also fortunate to have a wonderful family, Iqtedar, Arshia, Imtiaz, Danish and Rana. My children, Rumi and Ruhi, through their beauty and innocence and their unlimited reservoir of delights, remind me every day of the infinite debt that I owe to Allah (swt). I have received a lot of love from many, but two uncles deserve special mention. Their constant intellectual challenge played a major role in my development as a child. I thank Dr. Majeed Khan and Qazi Anees.

There are two individuals without whose support and friendship this book would never be a reality. They are Dr. John Esposito, my teacher and my friend and I owe him much, and Dr. Jamal Barazinji, a friend and guide, who brought this boat safely into the harbor. I wish also to thank the anonymous reviewer for meticulous feedback that helped improve the book and Dr. Fathi Malkawi for his encouragement. I am also grateful to Dr. Akbar Ahmed for his support and for writing the foreword to this book. I want to also thank Dr. Stan Caine, the president of Adrian College and my colleague and friend Professor Kim Davis for their support and encouragement, especially in the aftermath of September 11. Dr. Mohiaddin Mesbahi continues to remain a friend who cares and guides.

The book includes revised essays that have been published earlier. I would like to specially thank the Washington Report on Middle East Affairs, Mirror International, Muslim Observer, Detroit News, Detroit Free Press, and The Globalist who have helped make my voice heard over the cacophony of voices that now crowd our public spheres. I would also like to alert the readers that I have decided to rely extensively on the translations of the *Qur'an* by Abdullah Yusuf Ali, M. Pickthall and M. Shakir. All citations are from Yusuf Ali except those identified as taken from Shakir or Pikhtal. I chose three rather than a single translation to prevent one individual's reading of the Qur'an from dominating my thinking.

Needless to say, all the errors are from me, and *Wallahu Alam* (Allah knows best).

Muqtedar Khan, Ph.D.
Adrian, Michigan,
May 2002.

Chapter 1
Islam in America

The Manifest Destiny of American Muslims

We have made you a nation justly balanced.
– Qur'an 2: 143

In the last three decades, the American Muslim community has developed at an astonishing pace. Through conversions, immigration and natural growth it has grown in numbers and is now estimated to be between 6-8 million, making it the second largest religious community in the U.S. It has also grown in diversity. For a long time Arabs, South Asians and African Americans were the dominant groups in the community. More recently, Hispanic and Caucasian Muslims combine with the children of immigrant Muslims to enhance the diversity of American Muslims.

During these years of numerical growth, the overriding goal of American Muslims was to defend their Islamic identity. The transition of America itself from a melting pot to a multicultural society was a product as well as a facilitator of this resistance to assimilation. As the community became more organized and confident, it took up the struggle to gain recognition in mainstream America and fight the irrational fear of Islam and Muslims that is widespread. To a large extent Muslims have succeeded in challenging prejudiced perceptions of Islam and with significant help from a growing body of American scholars of Islam, like John Esposito of Georgetown University. Together they have managed to educate American media and governmental institutions about Islam and Muslims. New Muslim organizations such as Council for American and Islamic Relations (CAIR) and the American Muslim Council (AMC) have successfully joined the battle against prejudice and discrimination.

Before September 11, most Americans saw Muslims not as terrorists threatening peace or democracy, but as fellow God-fearing Americans, struggling to balance the challenges of modern/postmodern life with the imperatives of faith. Muslims are doctors, computer scientists, basketball players, professors and their next-door neighbors. The growth of white and black Muslims was also helping in convincing Americans that Islam was now an American faith and being Muslim was part of the American experience.

However the tragic events of September 11 and the fear and paranoia they have generated have set Muslims back. America before September 11 was on the verge of accepting Islam as one of its own but after the attacks it has paused to once again reassess Islam and Muslims. Since the attacks more and more Americans have started studying Islam and exploring the American Muslim community. The media has vastly increased its coverage of Islam and American Muslims and most of the coverage has been positive. The Message that Islam is a peaceful religion and that most American Muslims have the same aspirations as other Americans has been voiced strongly.

There is a new mood in America. The anti-Islam rhetoric is receding. Both the Congress and the White House have acknowledged Muslim presence and have allowed them some opportunity to give policy input; a privilege which many Muslims do not enjoy in most Muslim countries today. As a consequence of these successes, American Muslims have begun to believe in a manifest destiny of their own. The American Muslim community believes that it has a divine mission to fulfill. Its enormous intellectual talent, its highly educated population, the free and even encouraging environment of the U.S. and the enthusiasm and dynamism of Islamic resurgence, all combine to give the American Muslim community an excellent opportunity to not only spread Islamic values in the West but also influence and reshape the destiny of traditional Muslim societies. In a rather curious way the tragic events of September 11 have also helped bring American Muslims into the mainstream of American life and increasingly the government and media are seeking their input.

Life in America presents two distinct challenges to Muslims; one, the struggle to overcome prejudice against Islam, and two, the challenge of modernity and the stress it puts on traditional understanding and interpretation of Islamic values. Thus, building a Muslim community in America entails a two level game – dealing with challenges from outside and from within. While some Americans fear Islam, some Muslims too fear modernity and democracy. Muslims fear that the American way of life would undermine their Islamic identity. In the last three decades, American Muslims have dealt with the dual dilemmas most admirably. Thanks to enlightened activism by Muslim intellectuals and organizations and American openness and tolerance, not only has America come to accommodate Islam, many Muslims too have adjusted to modernity.

American Muslims have realized that if Islam has to survive in a fashion that makes it central and relevant to all spheres of human life, then it must learn to adapt as well as survive in the challenging environment of the West. The dangers to Islam in the present Muslim world are crude and physical. Islamists may face repression from secular authoritarianism, but the security agencies of these regimes are no substitutes for Islam. Islam therefore survives and will continue to remain central to Muslim life in the traditional Muslim world.

But in the West, the combination of liberalism, democracy and respect for diversity in conjunction with prosperity, present a real challenge to Islam. If it can be demonstrated that Islam is not only relevant but also necessary for a good and virtuous life in spite of the attendance of democracy and freedom, then Islamic values will be truly globalized and Islam will not be in danger of becoming anachronistic.

This then is the manifest destiny of American Muslims – to demonstrate to the rest of the world the relevance of Islamic values to a modern/postmodern society. By interpreting Islam such that it facilitates a virtuous existence, here and now, they can convince the West that Islam will only enrich it and also show the Muslim world how to walk the talk of Islamization.

If anything, the rise of Islamic militancy in many parts of the Muslim World compounds the challenge that American Muslims face. Increasingly there is a call from the West as well as from Muslims for a definition of moderate Islam. The task of not only articulating but also manifesting a moderate, peaceful, tolerant, inclusive, compassionate and moral model of Islam falls on the American Muslim community. It is because American Muslims live in relative freedom and prosperity that it is their duty, more than those of Muslims living either in poverty or subjugation, to realize the true essence of Islam and display – not just speak – the tolerance, the compassion and the inclusiveness that underpins the universal principles of Islam.

American Muslims as *Mujaddid*

Verily never will Allah change the condition of a people until they change it themselves. – Qur'an 13: 11

American Muslims cannot realize their destiny unless they actively imagine themselves as agents of change. Historically within Islamic traditions, agents of change have repeatedly struggled against the moral decay of society and the corruption of Islam. This mantle is ours to don and if American Muslims will take the imitative, they can provide leadership to the rest of the beleaguered *Ummah*. The Muslim world cannot continue to exist in its present condition. Change is necessary. Can American Muslims become an agent for change? I believe they can play the role of a *Mujaddid*.

The agency of *Mujaddid* has been a powerful influence on contemporary Islam. Revival (*Tajdid*) and reform (*Islah*) are Islam's internal mechanics for self-purification and for the periodic transcendence of its corporate self. A tradition that has the responsibility of safeguarding the Muslim *Ummah* (community) from deviating too much from the principles and practices of the Islamic faith. This tradition has become the philosophic foundation for anchoring and justifying efforts towards contemporary Islamic revival and reform. The *Mujaddid* (the reviver) is the central personality and also the main theoretician who leads the effort to revive Islamic values and to reconstruct Muslim society.

According to a tradition (*Sunna*) of Prophet Muhammad (pbuh), a *Mujaddid* will come at the beginning of every century in order to arrest the decline of Islamic practices and to revive the adherence to Islamic values and principles. This same *Mujaddid* is also a reformer since there can be no revival without reform. Thus *Tajdid* and *Islah* are concomitant.

Ijtihad, the use of independent reasoning and reinterpretation of The *Qur'an* and Islamic traditions, is the standard tool of the *Mujaddid*. *Ijtihad* is an important epistemological vehicle within Islam that protects it from stagnation, irrelevance and anachronism. In *Ijtihad*, the reviver finds the empowerment that allows her to revitalize Islamic beliefs by contextualizing them – by relating Islam to the immediate existential conditions of Muslims.

By reinterpreting reality through Islamic lenses and simultaneously reinterpreting the sacred texts with a steady eye on contemporary conditions, the *Mujaddids* systematically reduce the distance between text and time, between reason and revelation, between conscience and consciousness, between the here and the hereafter and between values and politics. In the contemporary *Mujaddid*, the three functions of revival (of values), reform (of society) and reinterpretation (of texts), have merged to create a powerful persona that has the potential to transform the nature of world politics and history.

The transformative capacity of this agent can be fully understood by merely looking at the achievements of Ayotollah Khomeini who personified this concept in our times. He not only led the successful Islamic revolution but also was instrumental in systematically transforming Iranian society. Other contemporary Muslims who have been identified as *Mujaddids* include, Maulana Maududi of South Asia who started the *Jamaat-e-Islami* (Islamic Society) an Islamic movement with great influence in India, Pakistan, Bangladesh, U.K. and Saudi Arabia, and Hassan al-Bannah of Egypt who launched the Islamic movement called *Ikhwan al-Muslimeen* (Muslim Brotherhood) that has branches and parallel movements in nearly the entire Arab world.

One of the challenges that *Mujaddids* from Ibn Hanbal to Maududi, had to contend with is the use of the state's repressive machinery as a deterrent to change. While the *Mujaddid* is essentially struggling to reform and bring change in the discourses and practices of his community, he nevertheless has to contend with the institutions of state and the distribution of power in his society. Ideally, a *Mujaddid* can be more successful, if he is allowed to work in a coercion free environment. This also can preclude the politicization of reform. But unfortunately since social practices are so deeply entwined with the production, distribution and exercise of power, a *Mujaddid* is always a political threat to the status quo. Often this *status quo* is the ruling alliance between the political elite and religious elite who legitimize each other.

Given the fact that the present Muslim World remains deeply antagonistic to change and reform, the hope of Islamic revival and reform is transferred to the Diasporas in the relatively freer environment in the West. We also live in a world that is far more complex than ever before. In such complex times, no single individual can play the role of a *Mujaddid* by him/herself. The role will have to be played by a community, a movement or at least a group. Towards this end, the responsibility of playing the role of the *Mujaddid* in the present century falls on the American Muslim community, which is best suited, both in terms of opportunity and ability. Let's hope that Muslims in America can come together to realize and fulfill this calling.

The ability of American Muslims to bring out change will first and foremost depend on their ability to provide a new and more moderate discourse. The American Muslim perspective must be authentic and original and not a mere echo of the voices from the traditional Muslim lands.

Have Muslims Arrived in America?

Establish justice and balance. – Qur'an 55: 9

Muslim search for authenticity and self-identity is often seen and portrayed by some Muslims and non-Muslims as an anti-West movement threatening its core interests. However, Muslims have arrived in America, but the substantive content of their arrival is far from such fears. Muslims have arrived in the U.S., but not as enemies of democracy and freedom but as full participants in American democracy, relishing as well as defending its freedoms.

In the year 2000, for the first time in American history, both the Republican as well as the Democratic national conventions for the formalization of the two parties' Presidential candidates began with prayers by Muslims. The Republican convention was kicked off by a

'*Dua*' (Islamic prayer) by Talat Othman, the Chairman of the Islamic Institute, and a '*Dua*' by Dr. Maher Hathout blessed the Democratic convention.

This dual recognition underscores not only the openness of the American system, but importantly it indicates the growing political influence of American Muslims. At the Republican convention that year, there were over one hundred Muslim delegates. A remarkable achievement for a community that is still debating whether it is permissible to participate in American politics. Once an internal consensus is achieved, the community with its current numbers and resources has the potential to become one of the most powerful domestic groups. The post September 11 developments, particularly the new laws which have to great extent put the civil liberties of American Muslims in jeopardy has further underscored the urgent need for Muslims to participate in American politics.

It is obvious that the momentum in favor of engaging in democratic politics is increasing within the American Muslim community. Not only are more and more Muslims registering to vote, Muslims are also actively engaging in politics on behalf of both the major parties. In other full and partially democratic societies like India, South Africa, UK and Singapore, Muslims who are in minority are politically active and full participants in systems that give them opportunity to express and defend their special interests.

Very rarely are the twin questions; Are Islam and Democracy compatible? And Can Muslims participate in the political systems where non-Muslims are in majority even discussed by the above-mentioned Muslim communities. While Islamic political theory lags far behind, Muslim practices on these issues are setting the trend. With American Muslims joining in, it is becoming apparent that "in custom" democracy has become acceptable to Muslims. At this point, one must remember that "*urf*", or custom, has always played a major roll in the development of Islamic legal discourse (*fiqh*).

Muslim intellectuals have so far not been able to advance a widely acceptable model of Islamic politics for our age. Nevertheless it appears as though Muslims are recognizing the immediate benefits of political engagement and are moving forward.

While it may not be clear whether democracy as practiced in the West is representative of how an Islamic polity would look in our times, we do realize that Islam advocates universal participation. All Muslims are enjoined to do good and avoid evil and struggle (*Qur'an* 9: 112) to establish justice and order on earth (*Qur'an* 4: 135). If participation through democratic politics gives Muslims in non-Muslim societies an "easy opportunity" to make some difference in the right direction, then they should not hesitate to play an active role in realizing this goal.

It is not necessary that theory should always precede practice. I am positive that the initiatives taken by the American Muslim community in the interest of Islam and the well being of Muslims will also pave open new directions of research and inquiry for Islamic political theory. Yes, Muslims have arrived and America and Islamic thought, both, will never be the same, ever again.

American Muslims and the Moral Dilemmas of Citizenship

Fulfill their treaty to them till their term. Lo! Allah loveth those who keep their duty. – Qur'an 9: 4 [Pickthall]

The occasional demonization of Islam in mainstream American media compels Muslims to become sensitive about their identity. All their activities are motivated by this sensitivity and are geared toward defending their faith from a perceived American assault. This phenomenon culturally and politically alienates as well as marginalizes observant Muslims.

Similarly the negative image of America in the eyes of many American Muslims, a consequence of its foreign policy in the Middle East, elicits paradoxical responses from American Muslims. America's prosperity and freedom attract them and, once they are here, its policies and its attitudes toward Muslims and Islam alienate them. Becoming American citizens presents an unusual moral dilemma for American Muslims. They love to live in America, while many of them love to hate America.

I once asked a Muslim leader at a seminar in Washington, DC to spell out the obligations of naturalized Muslim citizens to their new country – America – keeping in mind the Qur'anic injunction (*Qur'an*; 9: 4) that promises made must be kept. When one becomes a naturalized citizen one promises to be loyal and committed to the nation and its constitution.

While asserting that he was not an Islamic scholar and therefore unqualified to give an authoritative answer, this prominent American Muslim leader proceeded to give an interesting reply.

He said that, in the opinion of many scholars whom he had consulted, becoming a citizen should be understood as signing of a treaty between a Muslim individual and the United States. Therefore all Muslims who make this compact with the U.S. are obliged to fulfill their obligations as proper citizens, obey the law, pay taxes and so on. He also recommended that since the U.S. has offered the option to decline military draft to new citizens, Muslims could take this option to save themselves moral dilemmas if called to fight against Muslim states. If for some reason, he said, Muslims do not like the society of the United States they must terminate their treaty and leave.

However, he added, "of course Muslims are not obliged to obey laws and policies which are specifically against Islamic beliefs." He also recognized the opportunity for dissent and change that the U.S. constitution provides its citizens and recommended that Muslims avail themselves of this opportunity.

To most Muslims in the audience, the answer seemed rational, sensible, and even enlightened. Nevertheless, I was personally not very satisfied with his analysis. When Muslims become naturalized citizens they do not inform the U.S. government that their acceptance of U.S. citizenship is conditional. They do not make it clear to the U.S. that they will remain good citizens only as long as no explicitly anti-Islamic law or policy is legislated or implemented.

I am sure that the U.S. government would not agree to any such conditions, since after all it is the Muslim individual who is seeking association (citizenship) and not vice versa. Thus many Muslims who see Islam and the U.S. in a state of conflict have enormous problems in beginning to think of themselves as American Muslims.

They want the prosperity and the freedom of America, but not its foreign policy or its liberal culture. And Muslim leaders who oppose political assimilation without opposing naturalization inadvertently place Muslims in a morally delicate situation.

There are no simple solutions to this moral dilemma. It will have to be resolved at the theological level. Changes in American attitudes and policies toward Islam and Muslims will also be helpful in this transition to citizenship within the mind of each American Muslim. The theological discussion will have to take American Muslims beyond the *dar-ul-Islam* (house of peace) and *dar-ul-harb* (house of war) dichotomy.

The disappearance of the institution of the Caliphate, the emergence of many Muslim states – articulated as Islamic (Saudi Arabia, Iran, Pakistan, Sudan, Afghanistan) or as secular democracies (Turkey, Egypt, Malaysia, Indonesia) – and the rapid globalization of the nation-state as a result of decolonization have allowed many new terms to be invented within Muslim discourses on international relations.

These are words like *dar-ul-aman* (house of order) and *dar-ul-kufr* (house of unbelief). The term *dar-ul-aman* emerged in the context of Muslim politics in India.

India, which is a secular democracy and allows Muslims complete freedom to practice their religion and live by Islamic *Shariah* (law), cannot be labeled *dar-ul-harb* since it is not hostile to Islam. Since it does not have any specific treaties with obligations to Muslims it does not qualify as *dar-ul-sulh* (house of treaty). So, increasingly, Muslims have begun to refer to India and such countries as *dar-ul-aman*, house of order, where there is peace and tolerance and freedom of religion. But this term has been restricted to India in its use, perhaps because of its sub-continental origins.

Dar-ul-kufr is a state or territory which is predominantly non-Muslim but which neither has a treaty with Muslims nor is at war with them. The West has often been referred to as *dar-ul-sulh* , and by some as *dar-ul-kufr* depending upon political contingencies.

Those groups who wish to emphasize conflict between Islam and the West choose to describe the West as *dar-ul-kufr*, and those who choose to emphasize the peaceful and cooperative relations between Islam and the West call it *dar-ul-sulh.* These terms are also used in similar political discourses with respect to America.

Many American Muslims, particularly the African-American Muslims, are proud to be American citizens. They are indigenous to America and Islam has given them the dignity and self-esteem to make their lives meaningful, even as they struggle against racial discrimination.

Immigrant Muslims who share their sentiments are grateful for the opportunity that America has given them to prosper and practice their faith. They believe that America is *dar-ul-sulh* and that America, in many of its practices, is much more Islamic than many contemporary Muslim states.

Some immigrants, however, are of the opinion that since this is a country where Islamic *Shariah* is not applied, it is *dar-ul-kufr,* the house of unbelief. In my opinion this position is held by a minority of Muslims (from both indigenous and immigrant Muslims), but this minority is more active in Muslim politics and has a disproportionate impact on the American Muslim discourses.

Muslims must realize that there are legal procedures for change of law as well as policy in America and they must use it to pursue their self-interests. However, when they do become citizens and give the oath of allegiance to America to become a part of its community, they must do so in good faith and a clear conscience and awareness of what they are committing to. To be two faced, become citizens and enjoy rights but have no intention to fulfill the duties that come along is unjust, unfair and unIslamic.

Islamic Identity and the Two Faces of America

Let not the hatred of others to you make you swerve to wrong and depart from justice. Be just: that is next to piety:
– Qur'an 5: 8

The citizenship dilemma is a manifestation of the dialectic between Muslim identity and the Western influence. The contemporary resurgence of Islam and the growth of Islam in the West together have profound implications for what being a Muslim means today. The resurgence of Islam is essentially a search for authenticity, an attempt to reconstruct the Islamic identity within the contemporary context. And the said contemporary context remains within the purview of Western influence.

Muslim intellectuals and thinkers have all had to contend with the power of the West and the power of Western ideas while interpreting and understanding the condition of the Muslim *Ummah*. Many of them openly admired the West for its achievements in the arena of civil society as well as science and technology and have even remarked that the West was "Islam without Muslims". For them the West was indeed worthy of emulation in many areas such as democracy, human rights, and respect for the rule of law and for their dedication to science. This conception of the West has resulted in a genre of literature widely known as Islamic modernism when the theory of modernization was popular. Now in the age of liberalism, this Islamic tendency is referred to as Islamic liberalism.

Other Muslim thinkers have found the West responsible for the moral and material decline of the Muslim World. They blame Western imperialism and the era of colonial domination for the present backwardness and lack of self-government in the *Ummah*. They imagine it as the embodiment of Satan and have postulated Islamization as complete rejection of all that they see as Western, including democracy and freedom of speech. These thinkers are widely represented as Islamic fundamentalists in the West and are often contrasted with Islamic liberals. Needless to say, both discourses have an element of truth in them but both suffer from a lack of balance. While the former suffers from a lack of self-esteem and exaggerates the virtues of the West, the latter confuses polemics and diatribe against the West for Islam. Both elements are to some extent valid and even necessary but only as supplements to a dominant discourse that is both balanced and constructive.

The West is essentially like a Centaur – half human and half beast. The human face of the beast allows the West to appreciate the virtues of democracy, equality and freedoms of speech and religion. It provides it with the moral basis for protecting and treating its own citizens with utmost respect and dignity while also striving hard to advance their interests – understood in terms of political and material development. The bestial dimension of the West has led it to commit huge crimes against humanity. The World wars, the holocaust, colonialism, imperialism, slavery and racism are just a few of the crimes that the West has and/or to a much lesser extent continues to commit outside its borders. These elements of the West are puzzling. How can a society that has so much respect for the human life at home be so determined to allow the steady elimination of innocent Iraqis? How can a society that stands for equality and democracy allow so little freedom to other societies to disagree with it?

Today in an era of globalization, all civilizations are forced to live in intimacy. Also, millions of Muslims now live in the West and many others live in a close embrace of the Western ways of life. Understanding the puzzle that is the modern West is essential because its enormous power, both material as well as cultural has attained hegemonic proportions. There is very little resistance, except from some Islamists and some Asianists, to the growing influence of the West on the cultural and moral fabric of this planet.

We not only have to understand the modern West in a more balanced way and also develop a discourse for the reconstruction of Islamic identity that is neither weakened nor distracted by the enormous shadow of the West. Until we as Muslims can go beyond blind imitation of the West or outright rejection of its values, we will not be able to construct an Islamic self, independent of Western influence. It is essential that we develop a positive and constructive understanding of the "other". Only through such a positive and creative act will we be able to reconstruct a vibrant and meaningful self.

It is, therefore doubly important that Muslims in the West develop a "first hand" understanding of what the West really is. It is rather ridiculous that Muslims who have been living in the U.S. for decades put aside their own experiences and in order to understand the West, turn to the polemics of Muslim intellectuals of the sixties who have not experienced the contemporary West.

Only those who have had a sustained experience of the West and have witnessed both its human and its bestial dimension can develop a meaningful understanding of it. Others will continue to rely on caricatures, one way or the other.

What does it mean to have a balanced view of the West? It means that we do not throw out the baby with the bath water. Because Muslims are upset that the U.S. extends uncritical support to Israel and has imposed sanctions that kill Iraqi children, we must not reject democracy, human rights, respect for freedom and the rule of law.

A balanced view of the West should recognize the material impulses that shape many of the Western foreign policy choices and resist as well as condemn them. But in an endeavor to resist the Western domination we must not foolishly reject the laudable results of their moral impulses manifest so elegantly in their self-governing, rights respecting societies.

A balanced view of the West will rise far above simple associations. Because democracy is found in the West it should not be labeled Western. Now we can find Islam in the West too, does that mean Islam too is Western? A balanced view of the West will seek to understand the sources of Western values and also their implications to social welfare before passing judgment upon them. A balanced view of the West is essentially a considered and enlightened opinion of Western institutions and practices that does not allow negative emotions to cloud one's rational faculties.

A balanced view of the West will deconstruct extremist caricatures of the West that proliferate in the Muslim world. It will also desist from labeling the West as an anti-Islamic confederation of Jews and Christians but essentially recognize it for what it is – a multi religious, multiethnic and multicultural conglomerate that has rapidly become a microcosm of the whole world. While criticizing Western imperialist tendencies a balanced view will also emphasize the Western struggle to uphold democracy, gender equality and human rights.

Only when such an attempt to understand the West is made by Muslim intellectuals as well as the general public will the basis of a healthy Islamic identity emerge. Until then, reactions to the West will continue to subvert the construction of Islamic identity. And the responsibility of advancing such an understanding is the communal obligation of the Muslims of North America and Western Europe.

American Muslims: Global or Tribal?

O mankind! We created you from a single (pair) of a male and a female, and made you into nations and tribes, that ye may know each other. – Qur'an 49: 13

One of the major achievements of Islam was its near instant unification of Arabia into a singular, cohesive and extremely effective political unit. Arabia, in the pre-Islamic period comprised of over 400 tribes, each vying with one another for economic benefits and military glory. The division of duties – which were seen as honorable – on a tribal basis during the *Hajj*, is one of the many manifestations of the primacy of tribal identity and origins. Genealogy was, and perhaps still is, very important to the Arabs. They could remember not only their own family trees, but also those of their camels. It was in this provincial society that the Prophet Muhammad cultivated a feeling of brotherhood and community of universal dimensions. He inspired, and enlightened the Arabs to transcend their parochial perspectives and to view humanity from a universal standpoint.

In drawing the boundaries between the believers and the unbelievers, he broke down the boundaries between various Arab tribes. While drawing a circle around the *Ummah* and designating it as *Dar-ul-Islam* – The House of Peace – he erased the battle lines between black and white, Arab and non-Arab. In essence, the Prophet launched a spiritual movement that completely annulled narrowly defined identities and taught his followers the message of universality.

It is my contention that one of the most significant elements of the revelation of Islam and the transformation of society is the transcendence of narrow identities. In other words, the journey to Islam is also a movement away from tribalism and towards universalism.

Tribalism is a characteristic of ignorance. It is indeed a pre-Islamic condition.

Unfortunately tribalism, the instinct to privilege identities based on ethnic and place-specific origins, has proved to be one of the greatest enemies of Islam. It can also be described as one of the greatest weaknesses of Muslims, regardless of place or time. Immediately after the deaths of the Prophet Muhammad, Abu Bakr (rah), the first *Khalifa*, had to militarily assert that primacy of Islam over tribalism. In fact his entire *Khilafah* was dedicated to this task. But the nemesis persisted. Soon Uthman (rah), the third *Khalifa*, was accused of nepotism. After the sad departure Ali Ibn Talib (rah), the fourth and the last of the rightly guided leaders of Islam, tribalism completely usurped political domination. This also heralded the end of democratic politics in the Muslim world. The recent history of Islam is a chronicle of the ills of tribalism: nepotism, authoritarianism, internal strife, decline of internal cohesiveness and external effectiveness, and the gradual decay of the moral fabric of society.

Tribalism, under a new name, nationalism, was celebrated and universally legitimized by the political reforms and philosophic renaissance in Europe. It became the constitutive character of modern political organization as well as the primary source of human identity and was exported to the Muslim world during the colonial experience. Only the "Mahdi's" battles against the British in the late nineteenth century in Sudan were fought in the name of Islam. Most other independence movements were fought under the banner of nationalism.

While thinkers like Jalaluddin Afghani and Muhammad Abduh were strongly opposed to imperialism, it was perhaps only Maulana Maududi of the sub-continent of India who vociferously denounced nationalism. He condemned it as the greatest disease to plague humanity and especially the Muslims. Maududi's arguments were extremely valid. While Islam taught the virtues of the universal, nationalism celebrated the particular. While Islam united, nationalism divided.

Consider the formation of Bangladesh. In essence it was an assertion that Bengali language and cultural identity was more important than Islamic unity. While one cannot deny the widespread prevalence of authoritarian tendencies and ethnic bigotry in Pakistan (so vulgarly displayed in the frequent riots in Karachi), which is cited as the primary motive for cessation of the Bengalis, the partition of Pakistan was one more battle won by tribalism against Islam. At every such moment, when ethnicity or geographic elements are privileged over Islam in the assertion or exercise of identity, to my mind, it is one more step towards the reversal of the Prophet Muhammad's work. It is a step backwards, from Islam to ignorance. And as I argued earlier, they are clearly accompanied by social ills such as intolerance, bigotry and human misery. Tribalism truly reveals the ugliest face of humanity. If this seems far-fetched and unfair, one merely has to look at the sectarian conflicts in Pakistan, Rwanda, Sudan and Afghanistan. The evidence is compelling.

Unfortunately Muslims in America are beginning to cluster along ethnic and racial lines. There seems to be a growing divide between immigrant Muslims and indigenous Muslims. While there is much talk about stemming this, there is very little action being taken to bring the two communities together. Yes, there is cooperation on some important issues, but the cooperation is more of an alliance than unification. Similarly there is a widening gap between the two large immigrant groups, Arabs and South Asians.

This divide is manifest in some of the prominent Islamic associations in North America. In America we have an opportunity to create a microcosm of an *Ummah*, but unfortunately our tribal instincts never seem to allow us to escape from the darkness of ignorance into the light of Islam. This situation also indicates that Muslims who are coming to the West are really bringing their provincial and narrow perspectives along rather than the message of "truth and universality" – the essence of Islam.

Once again the specter of tribalism, divisiveness, and internal strife has followed us across the oceans. This is a very dangerous phenomenon. Muslims, who claim to be Muslims and are sincere about their Islamic beliefs should shrug this transitory and superficial comfort and sense of security that accompanies the ethnic seduction and think long term. Many contemporary Islamic scholars believe that if anything good in the name of Islam is going to happen, then it is the Muslims in the West, liberated from poverty and political repression, who will precipitate it.

But in order to realize this hope we must all act and think universally and boldly. We must strengthen our ties while erasing the lines that some colonial power arbitrarily drew. If Islam has to rise from the West, then the Muslims will have to come out of their ghettoes, into the open, open their arms and embrace humanity. Tribalism should be eliminated. Remember the message of the Prophet Muhammad's last sermon in which he instructed us to transcend racial and ethnic perspectives. Think big. Think *Ummah*. Think bigger. Think humanity.

The Clash of Origins

And among his signs are the variations in your language and color and in that are signs for those who know.
– Qur'an 30: 22

A major manifestation of tribalism within the American Muslim community is the growing divide between immigrant and indigenous Muslims. The young Muslim community of America is facing a major challenge that is threatening to create a cleavage between indigenous and immigrant Muslims. The differences between the two communities have been simmering for quite sometime and the matter came to a head when a coalition of immigrant Muslim PACS decided to endorse George Bush's candidacy for President without the cooperation of African American Muslims.

It is important to understand that the endorsement of George Bush was not the cause but the last straw that broke the camel's back. African American leaders were upset and felt alienated from the rest of the American Muslims. They felt that by endorsing Bush immigrant Muslims had abandoned them in their struggle against racism and civil and economic inequalities. Most African American Muslims sadly recognized the fact that for many immigrant Muslims, particularly their leaders, "back home" was still more important than this society and the Muslims who live here.

Many of the leaders of the African American Muslim community however are not as charitable in their analysis. They are incensed by this authoritarian and insensitive decision and have decided to strike out on their own in their struggle for justice and equality in America. The result is the formation of MANA, Muslim Alliance of North America, as an institutional expression of their no confidence in the organizations created and operated by immigrant Muslims.

On April 22, 2001, eighteen indigenous Muslim leaders met in Philadelphia to establish MANA. The purpose of MANA as stated in its mission statement is "to pursue an agenda that reflects the points of view and experiences of the indigenous Muslims of North America and addresses their needs and aspirations." Imam Siraj Wahhaj, the elected leader of MANA, commented that "MANA is open to all Muslims but the focus of the Alliance is on the issues and problems that indigenous Muslims deal with in America. And by indigenous, we mean all Muslims raised here in America."

On April 21 an Executive Committee was elected, which included: Imam Siraj and Imam Talib, in addition to Luqman Abdul Haqq, Asim Abdur Rashid, Amir al-Islam, Ihsan Bagby, Zaid Shakir and Hamza Yusuf.

The responses to this development from the immigrant community were very cautious and do not reflect the crisis in the community. An AMC communiqué on the issue celebrates the establishment of MANA but takes great pain to show that MANA has been on the cards for sometime now and is the result of two years of efforts by indigenous Muslims. Unfortunately no attempt has been made by any major organization to address the growing rift between immigrants and indigenous Muslims.

The growing anger and resentment among African American Muslims will not go away if immigrant Muslims pretend that it does not exist. It is time the leaders from both sides of the aisle came forward to have meetings that will first let all sides vent their emotions and complains and then begin a process of reconciliation.

I spoke with several leaders from the African American community. Unfortunately only a few have granted me the permission to use their names. One of the most vocal person on the issue is Aminah McCloud, Associate professor of Islamic Studies at Depaul University in Chicago. She felt that the resentment against immigrants has been growing among African Americans. She was quite candid in providing a list of their grievances.

African American Muslims, she said, are finding that some immigrant Muslims in spite of their Islamic claims tend to differentiate in their dealing with indigenous Muslims. They treat black and white Muslims differently. When a white converts s/he is glorified and treated like a saint and paraded everywhere. They are immediately given important roles to play within the community. Their opinions, regardless of their competence, are respected more than others'. Even though there are African Americans who have acquired Islamic education from prominent Islamic institutions and have mastered Arabic, their opinions do not enjoy the same respect as those of lay white converts. Even white American Muslims complain about being treated as trophy Muslims. They too resent the special treatment they get from immigrants.

Professor McCloud, who was the only African American Muslim scholar/leader of the many I interviewed for this discussion, who had no problems about being identified, adds that there is a perception that immigrants manifest discrimination in their marriage strategies. Both Arab and South Asian men, when they marry across race, often marry only whites (specially blondes) and the African American community takes the near absence of any intermarriage between blacks and immigrants as an insult.

There seems to be a general feeling among immigrant Muslims that African American Muslims are lacking in their Islamic knowledge and conduct. This condescending attitude reflects in joint projects and mixed *shura* committees when African American opinions and ideas are ignored and marginalized.

The philanthropic and charitable endeavors of the rich immigrant communities and their organizations, clearly shows their lack of concern and interest for the plight and condition of their African American brethren. Many Islamic charities raise millions of dollars to send to foreign places but provide very little charity at home. This is another aspect that divides the two communities.

A more serious concern is the growing feeling among African Americans that immigrant Muslims with their narrow focus on U.S. foreign policy are weakening the prospects of establishing Islamic values in America and jeopardizing the future of the American Muslim community and their own children.

African American leaders are convinced that immigrant Muslim understanding of the American system is superficial and self-serving. By ignoring the American experience of indigenous Muslims they are depriving the American Muslims as a whole from the best possible leadership it can get from an integrated community. While immigrant leaders see the establishment of MANA as "division of labor" and not "division of the community" it nevertheless is a division of leadership talent and the preclusion of a wisdom that can come from the pooling of experiences and knowledges.

Indigenous Muslims, especially African Americans, are heralding the creation of MANA as an important step. One is however tempted to ask them about the existing institutions related with Imam Warith Deen Muhammad. Why didn't indigenous Muslims choose to strengthen his mission rather than start a new organization? Does this mean that even existing indigenous Muslim institutions were ignoring local Muslims?

There are no clear answers. The situation is messy like life itself. It is in these messy conditions that American Muslims must find a way to muddle through, helping each other, cooperating with each other and most importantly finding common ground in areas where they differ.

The creation of MANA is a challenge to indigenous as well as immigrant Muslims. MANA should not mean that indigenous Muslims isolate themselves from other Muslims and the Muslim World at large. They will have to prove that they can not only take care of their affairs, but given their claim that they understand the system better, they will have to show a greater ability to influence America on behalf of Islam.

For the immigrant community, MANA is a call for soul searching. We love to brag that there is no room for racism in Islam, is this true of our conduct too? Are we showing an inferiority complex towards whites and superiority towards blacks in the way we manage our affairs? If in spite of our Islamic credentials we discriminate, then why do we criticize America so much for its racism? Are we so deeply hypocritical? Are the accusations that we care little about things here and for the future of Islam in America true? If true, are we being true to our own children by ignoring American society and spending our resources on societies we have left behind? Is the future of our political goals more important than the spiritual future of our children?

In my interviews and discussions I have found that some of our senior leaders, because of their successes, have become very arrogant and less consultative. They seem to think that all decisions they make are right and they simply shrug criticism as inconsequential. It is time we also examined how seriously we take the Islamic values of *Shura* that we so regularly brag about. Every community must reflect on its soul in order that it continues on the straight path. It is time, now more than ever, for American Muslims to sit back on reflect on the future of Islam and Muslims in America with a critical eye on the way we have been functioning.

Achieving Political Unity Among Muslim Americans

And hold fast by the covenant of Allah all together and be not disunited. – Qur'an 3: 103 [M. Shakir]

The growth of Islam in America, driven by migration and conversions, has created a diverse and multicultural Muslim community. While many scholars are busy studying how this community is faring in the pluralist and multicultural environment of the U.S., very little attention has been paid to the rather interesting fact that the American Muslim community is itself a multicultural community. Composed of people from all races, and from nearly every country of the planet, American Muslims are rapidly becoming a microcosm of the global Muslim community. The politics of identity and identity formation that is shaping the American Muslim community cannot be fully understood until the internal diversity within the community itself is fully appreciated.

There are two issue areas that have the greatest impact on the identity formation, development and politics of the American Muslim Community – religious development and political goals. The American Muslim Community has been struggling to build Islamic institutions like mosques and Islamic centers, Islamic schools, and Islamic societies for *Dawah* and religious development of the community. In this endeavor they have succeeded to a great extent. Islamic organizations like the Islamic Society of North America (ISNA), Islamic Circle of North America (ICNA), and the Muslim American Society led by Imam W. D. Muhammad are well ensconced and are serving the community admirably. Today there are nearly two thousand Islamic centers and hundreds of Islamic schools that are also toiling to defend the erosion of Islamic identity as well as doing *Dawah* to sustain one of the fastest growing communities in the West.

But in the arena of American politics, American Muslims have yet to make an impact proportionate to their size and potential. In spite of the growth of Muslim organizations designed for political mobilization and education, Muslims have yet to enjoy the fruits of political victories. Like its markets, the political environment in the U.S. has very high entry barriers. But more than external barriers there are certain characteristics of the American Muslim community itself that have erected internal barriers to political cohesiveness and effective mobilization. The single most important barrier to political cohesion in the American Muslim Community is the inability of the community to prioritize its political goals and identify a widely acceptable short list of political goals.

The American Muslim community is composed of Muslims from many parts of the Muslim world, and with the growth of the community, many sub-groups have emerged. The biggest groups are those composed of Muslims from the Arab World and South Asia. Each sub-group is attempting to organize itself to pursue sectarian rather than the over all goals of the community. However, the community at large is fortunate to have among its midst many leaders who have a vision of a strong and cohesive American Muslim community and have to a great extent succeeded in preventing the fragmentation of the community.

The best example of a well-organized sub-group is the Pakistani-American Community. This group has as many political action committees as the American Muslim Community. While on Islamic issues, such as building mosques or Islamic schools, Pakistanis remain an integral part of the American Muslim Community. In regards to political issues they have sought to chart their own separate territory. One can understand that the political challenges that Pakistan faces affects Pakistanis more than it does other Muslims and they cannot afford to wait for American Muslims to become sufficiently powerful to deal with all political issues facing other sub-groups.

Major Muslim organizations are clearly more focused on Arab and Middle Eastern issues with the Palestinian issue often dominating and even determining the agenda of several organizations. For example all major American Muslim organizations have launched campaigns against the U.S. policy of sanctions in Iraq but have rarely raised the issue of sanctions against Iran. Iran has been a greater ally of American Muslim organizations on the subject of Palestine and Jerusalem than Iraq. It is truly a shame that American Muslims have done so little to create a rapprochement between Iran and the U.S.

Increasingly Muslim activists who are not of Arab ethnicity are expressing their tiredness with Arab issues including the Palestinian problem. After September 11, many African American, White, South Asian and West Indian Muslims have privately expressed that Islam and Muslims are suffering because of the Islamic militancy and extremism coming from the Arab world. Even though South Asia has its own share of Islamic extremists (Taliban for example), the presence of this group is also being blamed on Arab influence.

If all sub-groups pursue their own goals on their own, they will not only weaken the American Muslim community by redirecting resources, but they will also prevent the emergence of a cohesive American Muslim Community. The challenge facing American Muslims is the classic dilemma of collective action. If all subgroups cooperate in building strong political institutions of a unified American Muslim Community, these institutions will serve as a public good that will serve all their interests. A strong, well-established and funded American Muslim Community can have greater influence on issues than its smaller constituent communities on their own. But in order to create this powerful community, each subgroup must put a hold on their immediate sectarian ambitions in the interest of strengthening the American Muslim Community.

At present, many subgroups are reaching a critical mass that can enable them to have some rudimentary forms of separate institutions. The temptation to breakaway from the mainstream on political issues while cooperating on religious issues must be resisted in the interest of the larger community. If American Muslim leaders fail to prevent emerging subgroups from breaking away, the American Muslim community will become *a community of communities* rather than a singular multiethnic and multiracial community.

The task of achieving political unity is difficult since there are many interests, sometimes even competing interests, within the American Muslim community. It is going to be very difficult to get all Muslims to agree upon the same political goals. This will not happen until all Muslims in America have the same identity – American Muslim. As long as many of them continue to think of themselves as Arab American, African American and so on, there will be different interests and the community will remain divided. However, it is possible for enlightened American Muslim leaders to at least agree on one single goal – to strengthen the American Muslim community. Everything else will fall in place slowly as we wait for the next generation of American Muslims to grow up with more unified and more homogenous interests. So let us work together to strengthen our community – The American Muslim community. Let this be our common ground and our first priority. We can differ on our other priorities but unity can come only if our most important issue is genuinely a shared issue.

The challenges that American Muslims face in the aftermath of September 11 provide a rallying point for American Muslims to unite in pursuit of pure self-interest. It remains to be seen if the community can rise to the challenges it faces of fragmentation from within and marginalization from without.

Chapter 2

American Muslims
and American Politics

Democratic trends among American Muslims

*Had Allah willed He could have made you
one community? But that He may try you by that
which He hath given you (He hath made you as ye are).
So vie one with another in good works.*
– Qur'an 5: 48 [Pickthall]

The transition of American Muslims from a fragile group focused on defending its identity to an intrepid community determined to make an impact has not been without contention. There still is no consensus in the community over several issues. To understand the political dynamics of the Muslim community it is essential that one understand its two main factions: "Muslim Democrats" (Muslims who are concerned with American democracy) and "Muslim Isolationists" (those who focus primarily on American foreign policy).

These two groups cooperate fully on practical issues concerning the defense of Islamic identity, such as establishing and maintaining Islamic centers and schools. Seen in this context, the community appears to be seamless. On political issues, however, these two groups break apart and disagree on many issues. It may be safe to say that, while the two groups have common ground in preserving Islamic belief and rituals, they represent completely different conceptions of the role of Muslims in America.

Muslim isolationists see the U.S. government as an evil empire dedicated to global domination. They have seen how U.S.-led sanctions have gradually squeezed the life out of Iraq, killing hundreds of thousands of Muslim children. Recently they watched in horror as Israeli Army killed more than 2000 protesting Palestinians using a war machine built in part with U.S. aid of some $4 to $6 billion a year, totaling more than $80 billion. They are amazed that the U.S., the self-proclaimed defender of human rights, does not admonish its ally Israel. Muslim isolationists are incensed with the U.S. for its utter disregard for Muslim lives and Muslim society, and the American media's demonization of Islam and defamation of Muslims.

Most importantly, Muslim isolationists are unimpressed with America's democracy or its values of freedom and pluralism. They see American society as immoral, sexually decadent, greedy and exploitative of the weak at home and abroad. For them democracy is an institution that legitimizes the basic instincts of humanity and thus is an affront to divine laws. Describing the American system as "*kufr*" (a system against the laws of Allah or the Islamic *Shariah*), they reject it totally.

Muslim isolationists reject all that is American and Western. The frustration and animosity they feel as a result of American foreign policy excesses is translated into a rejection of all that is American and Western, including democracy and religious tolerance.

There is an element of hypocrisy, too, in the manner in which the isolationists conceptualize their own role in America. They maintain that since the American system is not divinely ordained and is not geared toward realizing the Islamic *Shariah* (ignoring the fact that, in theory, both the American constitution and the Islamic state seek justice, protection and the moral and material well-being of their citizens), participation in that system violates Allah's decree in the *Qur'an* (5: 45) that Muslims shall not rule by anything other than what Allah has decreed. Since participation, they argue, equals endorsement of the system, they are therefore opposed to Muslim participation in American politics.

Even though they reject the entire political system, they have no qualms about participating in the American economy. They take up jobs, pay taxes (to support the system), and some of them even start businesses in the system where, like the polity, the economy also is un-Islamic. The isolationists argue that American Muslims must participate only in an effort to revive the institution of *Khilafah*, which magically will take care of all Muslim problems. Some of the isolationists have organized themselves under the banner of *Hizb-ul-Tahreer,* a fringe political movement that advocates a narrow and harsh interpretation of Islam. *Tahreer* has been shut down in majority of Muslim countries, most recently in Pakistan. In fact, the only places where *Tahreer* adherents are free to pursue their activism in the open and without any fear of state reprisal are in the West. Ironically, then, *Tahreer* condemns the West for its belief in democracy and freedom, yet it is this very belief in freedom that has helped them avoid political extinction. In the last few years, the isolationists have focused their attention on preventing Muslim democrats from bringing their co-religionists into the American mainstream. Their attempts to create intellectual and political ghettos have failed as more and more Muslims are beginning to participate in the American political process.

On the other hand, Muslim democrats not only have transformed American Muslims from a marginal, inward-looking immigrant community to a reasonably well-organized and coordinated interest group, able not only to fight for its rights but also to begin asserting its interests at the national as well as international level. Their real significance, and the key to the Muslim democrats' success, has been their understanding of the West and their liberal vision of Islam. Muslim democrats were quick to grasp the significance of the American Constitution's guarantee of religious freedom. They used this initially to organize institutions and movements solely focused on preserving the Islamic identity of Muslims.

As more and more Muslims came to America and answered their rallying call, Muslim Democrats began to see a dream: a dream of a "model Muslim community" practicing Islam as well as playing a leadership role, guiding not only other Muslim communities but all Western societies toward a life of goodness and God-consciousness. Muslim democrats see in America not only the imperialist impulse, but also its respect for law and fellow human beings. They are aware of the West's double standards in treating its own citizens and others differently. This was not new to them, since they have witnessed their own societies employing similarly separate standards. Of course Muslim democrats are frustrated with the U.S. when it does not fulfill its commitments to democracy and human rights in the Muslim world. They are quick to acknowledge, however, that Muslims are better treated here than in their native countries. Having seen democracy, pluralism, and cultural and religious tolerance in action, they are fascinated by America's ability to peacefully resolve political differences, as well as the problems of collective actions.

They admire the U.S. for its commitment to consultation and its desire to rule wisely through deliberation, and wish that Muslim societies, too, could escape the political underdevelopment from which they currently suffer and rise to manifest Islamic virtues.

Muslim Democrats have had three major successes. Firstly, they were able to quickly assume leadership positions in nearly every avenue of American Muslim activism. Whether in the political arena or in religious affairs, Muslim democrats hold sway. Secondly, they have been able to advance a vision for the American-Muslim community that makes its members proud of themselves and galvanizes them to contribute their money and time in the pursuit of this vision.

Their greatest achievement, however, has been their liberal interpretation of Islam. Through thousands of seminars, persuasive articles in monthly magazines and Islamic center newsletters, lectures at regional and annual conventions of ICNA, ISNA, AMC, CAIR, MSA and MYNA (Muslim Youth of North America), workshops and leadership retreats over the last 30 years, and Friday prayers across the nation, Muslim democrats have campaigned to alter the way Muslims think about America and about Islam itself. They have fought for the legitimacy of their ideas against traditional scholars and battled against the siege mentality that had prevented Muslims from opening up and taking a fresh look at the world and at their collective self.

During these three decades, Muslim Democrats have shifted the Muslim community's focus from battling the West to building bridges with it. They have rejuvenated the tradition of *ijtihad*, or independent thinking among Muslims, and now speak openly about *fiqh al-aqliat* (Islamic law, or interpretation of the *Shariah*, in places where

Muslims are in minority). They have emphasized Islamic principles of justice, religious tolerance and cultural pluralism. They have Islamized Western values of freedom, human rights, and respect for tolerance by finding Islamic sources and precedents that justify them.

In the run up to Election 2000 the struggle between the two categories of American-Muslim elites intensified. However, the isolationists may have succeeded too well – for they have been completely isolated. Muslim democrats, on the other hand, succeeded in mobilizing Muslims to register to vote, and American Muslims voted in large numbers, making a difference in the crucial state of Florida. Today American Muslims are not only eager to participate and make an impact – they have made an impact already.

The isolationists have no program or vision that would attract Muslims. They themselves spend their resources attacking Muslim democrats for "inventing an American Islam." Their activism now is limited to harassing Muslim activists and trying to place hurdles in their paths.

As a new generation of Muslims joins the community, the influence of Muslim Democrats is consolidated. While the new generation is familiar with the problems of the Muslim world and its bill of complaints against the West, life, as they know it is in the West, with all its pluralities and inconsistencies. They are strongly in the corner of the democrats and are proud to be Muslim and American – for they are American Muslims. They believe in Islam, they are democratic, they respect human rights and animal rights and share the concern for the environment. They are economic and political liberals and social conservatives. They believe in freedom of religion and the right of all peoples, ethnic as well as religious, to be treated equally. They are aware of their economic and political privileges and grateful to Allah for them.

They dream of making changes in Muslim attitudes as well as Muslim conditions, so that their fellow Muslims also can experience the bliss of practicing Islam by choice, and without fear of the state or a dominant group.

Refutation of Isolationist Arguments

O ye who believe! Make not unlawful the good things that God hath made lawful for you.. – Qur'an 5: 87

It is my belief that arguments, which suggest that Muslims should not participate in American domestic politics, stem from ill informed and misconstrued notions about the nature of American polity. Here I will try to deal with some misconceptions about American government.

Muslims believe in Allah as the supreme legislator, and therefore isolationists argue that Muslims should not look up to the leaders of the West (political or religious) for guidance. The claim that Allah is the sole giver of Law and Islam forbids humans from assuming this role (that would amount to playing God) is the standard argument advanced against democracy and American form of government. The point being democracy is seen as the arrangement where Man (or his reason) is sovereign and therefore laws – moral, economic and political – are designed to advance convenience and not submission to Allah. Therefore, participation in the American political process tantamount to affirming human sovereignty rather than Allah's and is not permissible.

I contend that this argument is premised on a false understanding of the democratic process. Democratic process essentially implies the inclusion of all citizens in power sharing and in decision-making. Democracy is a safeguard from the problem of power being usurped by a small number of people who then legislate laws that advance their individual or group interests and employ the state as a tool for dominating the masses towards realization of these same partisan interests. Democracy's primary function is to empower the marginalized and to give a voice to those who have not had a say in determining their own destinies. Democracy is the operationalization of the principle of self-determination. If people determine to live by the principles of Islam then democracy is not a hurdle, it is a facilitator.

Democracies come in different forms. The British case is one where a theological state gradually became secular while remaining democratic during the transition and the present Turkey suggests that the reverse is conceivable. Both Maulana Maududi and Ayatollah Khomeini, a Sunni and a Shia political theorist of Islam, have envisaged a limited role for the democratic process.

Khomeini's "Vilayat-e-faqi" is a state where the knowledgeable, the righteous and the just rule in the name of Islam. They are the ones who will make explicit the Islamic *Shariah* according to the needs of the Islamic Republic. To Khomeini democracy would weed out the unjust and unrighteous *ulema*. For Maududi, theodemocracy would serve as the operationalization of the principle of *shura* (consultation). The elected legislature would merely derive Islamic laws from The *Qur'an* and the *Sunnah* and supervise its implementation. Democratic elections would serve the function of providing legitimacy. Maududi's theodemocracy is basically representative *shura*. Thus in an Islamic society when elected members of the *shura* council deviate from the straight path they lose out in the next election.

The Islamic concept of *Khilafah*, or vicegerency places political agency in the *Ummah*. Each and every member of the *Ummah* (Man and Woman) is Allah's vicegerent on earth and therefore empowered by Allah to act on his behalf in instituting his *Din*. It is this sovereign corporate, the *Ummah*, which selects/nominates/elects the Caliph (the difference in the spelling is to distinguish between the person and the concept) who then acts as the agent of Allah's agents. Given the large numbers of Muslim believers (over 1.4 billion) and the increased complexity of society, it would be difficult to conceive of any other means of electing the Caliph other than democratic means.

There are those who argue that Islam has a system of bayah. They are so stuck on terminology that they fail to see that swearing allegiance to a Caliph was feasible when there were a few thousand citizens. A plain yes or no on a piece of paper or even on the Internet would today serve the same purpose. The point is if we look at concepts and principles we find that democratic procedures are compatible with Islam.

I have extensively studied the concept of sovereignty in Islam and in Western political theory. I have found that rather than contradict Islam, many of the constitutive principles of sovereignty in the West are derived directly from Islam. Jean Bodin and Jean Jaques Rousseau, the two earliest and most prominent theorists of modern sovereignty derived their respective ideas of absolute sovereignty and popular sovereignty directly from Islam. Rousseau had made an extensive study of the Prophet Muhammad's (pbuh) rule in Madina to derive his ideas of sovereignty. Thus the shadow of Islam on the premises of popular governance and democratic theory is significant.[1]

Coming to the American democracy, its model is very similar to Maududi's theodemocracy. In America, the representative *shura* (The Congress) derives laws from the constitution. It at least seeks to legislate laws that do not contradict the constitution of America. Thus while Muslim legislators would in a Muslim democracy seek to implement and protect the *Qur'an* and *Sunnah*, the Americans implement and protect their constitution. Those critical of American democracy, often call it *kufr* and more, but they advance their judgments with very little or no analysis. Future discussions should directly examine the substance of the constitution and examine its convergence and divergence from Islamic values. A two-line condemnation may perhaps be a disservice to American Muslims.

Would we be satisfied if people read one or two books on Islam or read a book on Islam by non-Muslims and rejected it? Wouldn't we accuse them of being superficial and prejudicial in their rejection of Islam? Let us give others the same courtesy that we demand. Let us at least examine their position in its subtlest form before passing judgments. Hasty and uninformed judgments are mere indicators of ignorance and even intolerance. It will unnecessarily distance people from Muslims and Islam.

I am reproducing the preamble to the American constitution here to ask readers what is anti-Islamic or anti-God about it?

> *We the people of the United States, in order to form a more perfect Union, establish justice, secure domestic tranquility, provide for the common defense, promote the general welfare, and secure the blessings of liberty to ourselves and*

---

1. See Muqtedar Khan, "Sovereignty in Modernity and Islam," *East West Review*, Vol 1, (Summer, 1995) pp. 43-57.

our posterity, do ordain and establish this constitution for the United States of America.

I would like to know what is it in this preamble (the *maqasid* of the American constitution) that an Islamic state would not like to provide to its people. Does Islam seek to deprive Muslims of justice, domestic tranquility, welfare, liberty or prosperity? This may not be a constitution that explicitly states itself to be Islamic. How can it be? Remember Muslims choose to condemn it and stay away from it, its conception is Muslim free but not Islam free. There is much in it which is Islamic and what is unIslamic I leave it to its critics to point out. I assume they have read it and are intimately conversant with its drawbacks and fallibilities not to mention its unIslamic characteristics.

Islam can be realized in practice or it can be reduced to the status of a flag, a symbol, or a sticker. Muslims seem to be more interested in labels and external, visible, exhibition of Islam rather than institution and application of Islamic values. This does not mean that everything about America is Islamic. Certainly not. It is far from an ideal Islamic society and also far from what its own constitution stipulates. But at least America has its sights on a target, which is closer to the bulls-eye as compared to most Muslim societies that are far from their avowed social and political ideals and goals. This country, thanks to its values, treats Muslims better than most Muslim countries. Here we have more opportunity to practice Islam freely than in many parts of the Muslim world and it is in our interest to appreciate and defend this quality of America.

How Muslims can influence American Politics

Teach [about truth, justice, fairness, tolerance and about goodness], for teaching benefits the believers. – Qur'an 51: 55

Muslims must participate in American Politics. That question is settled. However, one must be very careful about how one plans participation in politics. Muslims cannot be just another ethnic group with special interests particularly in foreign policy, like Jewish-

Americans or Cuban-Americans. We are seeking change, not only in how the U.S. deals with Muslims overseas but also how American society evolves at home. After all, our children will grow up and live in this society and we must work as hard as possible to make it morally safe and materially satisfying.

Muslims must therefore enter politics as a normative element to enhance the good and forbid the evil. We should take the moral high ground, avoid partisanship and support, financially as well as politically (using our votes and checkbooks), all those who seek morally positive change, whether they are Democrats or Republicans.

We must become the conscience of America, its inner moral voice, so that we may safeguard our lives and protect it within the boundaries of Islam. This is a necessary step to ensure an Islamic future for our children and their children.

As Muslims, we can participate at several levels by first educating ourselves. We must find out what issues are driving the elections and ask ourselves, do these issues affect Muslim life here and overseas? We should write letters to the candidates, call their local representatives and demand that Muslim issues be included in their platforms. We can volunteer for our chosen presidential candidate and campaign within our local communities. We must get known and let America know that Muslims are here and they care about our shared future. We should write letters to the editors of our local newspapers, write emails to news organizations like CNN and MSNBC and express Muslim concerns and opinions of the candidates and their positions.

We should avoid wasting time and resources in arguing with those who call all these activities "*kuffar*" activities. These individuals subvert the activities of Muslims who are working to make a change.

Politics in America is at once simple as well as very complex. The domination of the two parties simplifies the ideological spectrum. If you are on the right, go with the Grand Old Party (GOP) and if you are on the left, go with the Democrats. Yes! Muslims can be on both sides of the aisle. Remember Amir Muawiyyah (rah), he was very much on the right. Remember Abu Dharr (rah), he was very much on the left.

But the freedom that politicians enjoy to vote their conscience brings complexity and unpredictability to the system and makes it very interesting. To navigate this unpredictability one needs to not only follow the issues very carefully, but also to follow the record of the politicians.

The good news is that the deliberation over policy issues has become more and more public and inclusive. Candidates participate in hundreds of town meetings to present their views and hear public opinion. Muslims must not only go to these meetings but also participate. Let them hear your concerns. Most importantly, let them know that you are there and are as powerful as any other American. Exercise your rights and demand that they accommodate your interests.

As a scholar and a teacher, I see the role of Muslims in American politics as one seeking to teach. First we must teach ourselves about the system and then participate in the system to teach the message of Islam. America is a great country but there is still a big gap between its values and its reality. We must work to bridge that gap. When we struggle for a better America, we struggle to ensure a better future for us and our children.

The Public Face of Bigotry

Not all of them are alike: of the People of the Book are a portion that stand [for the right]; they rehearse the signs of Allah all night long and then prostrate themselves in adoration. – Qur'an 3: 113

One of the areas where Muslim role in American politics can be beneficial is in the struggle against bigotry and pockets of intolerance that we witness in American politics on a daily basis.

All societies have their flaws. Some discriminate and others are intolerant of religious differences. Some societies call their fellow human beings as untouchables while others insist on limiting the public role of women. American society too has suffered from the persistence of anti-Semitism and racism. Yet what is remarkable about America is its self-conscious attempt to purge itself of its moral flaws. Since the civil rights movement in the early sixties and the simultaneous spread of liberal values, American society has struggled to eliminate all forms of bigotry from its public sphere without compromising on first amendment rights.

But occasionally, as it happened during the elections of 2000, whenever the fighting between Palestinians and Israelis escalates and after September 11, many nasty episodes have revealed the persistence of prejudice and bigotry in American public sphere. Large scale anti-Muslim prejudice has surfaced suggesting that Americans who are Muslims are a despised other that can be publicly maligned without fear of any moral or legal consequences.

Rick Keller the Republican candidate for Florida's 8th district, pompously declared (October 12), "I think Palestinians are lower than pond scum". Radio talk show personality Don Imus on October 17 called Arafat a "dish raghead". Reverend Graham Jr. attributed evil to Islam and a Louisiana representative insisted on referring to Arabs as those who wear towels on their heads. There have been several instances where people in responsible places have made irresponsible statements even thought President Bush and members of his staff have called for tolerance. The Council on American and Islamic Relations has done a great job of documenting anti-Islamic bigotry and anyone interested in details can contact them.

In a democracy political leaders and the news media are the guardians of social values. It is their responsibility to expose and weed out bigotry and prejudice from the society, not foster it. Bigotry is a function of ignorance and is usually found in the lower strata of society. But when the so-called elite, senate candidates to prominent newspaper columnists, themselves publicly indulge in bigotry, the moral fabric of the society itself is at risk.

All these acts of hate speech tell a sad story. America has yet to free itself from the tyranny of prejudice. The American elite is so keen to win or to register their viewpoint that they are capable of shedding all dignity and statesmanship and is ready to tread on the rights of those who may not be able to strike back.

Hate speech that operates freely in the public sphere acts as a cancer against the values of tolerance and pluralism. Every bigoted word uttered against Muslims or any other minority is a blow against democracy.

Was Endorsing Bush a Good Decision?

Allah's reward will be for those who conduct their affairs through mutual consultation. — Qur'an 42: 38

There were several reasons why American Muslims chose to unite behind George Bush in the Presidential elections. Chief among them was the perception that both Bill Clinton and Al Gore were too heavily invested with the Israeli lobby to adopt a balanced approach to the Palestinian issue. American Muslims felt that Bush would not only assume a more balanced attitude toward Palestinians but would also reduce the colonization of the peace process by American Jews. They felt that since all the important foreign policy positions were held by American Jews, such as the post of U.S. Ambassador to Israel held by Martin Indyk, who had a long history of lobbying for Israel, it was impossible to expect Democrats to be even-handed towards Palestine. American Muslims and Arab leaders believe that American evenhandedness is absolutely necessary for a fair and sustainable solution to the Arab-Israeli conflict.

While the Israeli lobby has failed to make any inroads into the Bush foreign policy setup, comments made by George Bush to the American Jewish Committee suggest that perhaps American Muslims' faith in George Bush might be misplaced. On May 4, 2002 President George W. Bush declared his administration "will be steadfast in supporting Israel against terrorism and violence, and in seeking the peace for which all Israelis pray."

"A top foreign policy priority of my administration is the safety and security of Israel," he added for good measure. "We will stand up for our friends in the world. And one of the most important friends is the State of Israel." Such words of assurance by Bush to American Jews sound very similar to the ones he uttered to American Muslims. The difference is that promises to Muslims were made before the elections and promises to American Jews are being made after the elections. American Muslims find this Bush posturing very difficult to understand or accept given the fact that while 78% American Muslims voted for Bush less than 20% American Jews voted for him.

After September 11, the White House has openly supported Israel and Ariel Sharon against the Palestinians and Arafat. Even though President Bush has called for a Palestinian State, his conditions are seen as supporting Sharon's occupation and as undermining Palestinian struggle for Statehood.

American Muslims thought they were making a breakthrough by uniting behind George Bush. Many American Muslim leaders, remembering only the fact that George Bush Sr. and Jim Baker were tough with Israel on the issue of settlements, hoped to see change in U.S. policy towards the Arab-Israeli conflict.

The new President has definitely instituted several changes in the U.S. approach toward the Arab-Israeli conflict but not exactly in the way American Muslims had hoped he would. The repeated bombing of Iraq by Bush within a few weeks of his inauguration was a sign that he had many surprises in store for American Muslims. Yes, visibly the influence of the Israeli lobby on the White House looks as if it has diminished. But both American Muslims as well as the Palestinians seem to have lost access to the American President. During Clinton's Presidency, not only did American Muslim organizations have access to the White House, but also Chairman Arafat accumulated an enviable amount of frequent flyer miles from his trips to Washington, DC.

American Muslims are not happy with the changes in the U.S. role vis-à-vis Palestine. The new role of the American President as a detached facilitator of peace rather than a deeply engaged negotiator of peace has paid no dividends at all. The American hands-off approach has meant that Palestinians have no recourse but to be at the mercy of the Israeli army. As settlements grow and Palestinian frustration rises, violence and pain continue unabated. While the American administration maintains that violence in Israel is largely the fault of Palestinians and Arafat's unwillingness to stop it, most victims are Palestinians.

Sharon has interpreted the hands-off approach of President Bush as license to use disproportionate amount of violence to break the Palestinian spirit. Tanks and helicopter gun ships are now used routinely by his forces. He has also escalated the rate of settlement building in occupied territories in direct violation of international law and the stated policies of the U.S. and the European Union. Washington has yet to express any condemnation of the continued building of Israeli settlements on Palestinian land. The American hands-off approach fits well with Ariel Sharon's aversion to making peace with Palestinians. Sharon would rather use Israel's military superiority to repress Palestinians than exchange land for peace.

The U.S. and the role it plays in the Arab-Israeli conflict is crucial for peace of any kind in the region. For the U.S. to be able to play the peace catalyst it must enjoy the trust and confidence of all parties involved. George Bush has succeeded in losing the trust and confidence of American Muslims who supported his candidacy, contributed to his campaign and voted en masse for him. American Muslims have found that he does not keep his promises and Palestinians have found that he does not care for their sufferings.

In the aftermath of September 11, American Muslims have discovered that a Republican in the White House is not exactly in their interest. They fear that perhaps the conservatives are using September 11 as an opportunity to pursue their anti-immigration policies more aggressively. While president Bush himself has been very sensitive to the fears and plight of Arab Americans and American Muslims, the Attorney General however has shown a great deal of enthusiasm in arresting hundred of Arabs and Muslims on flimsy charges and has also been very aggressive in his attacks on Muslim charities.

The decision taken by several American Muslim organizations to endorse Bush was not exactly a democratic decision. Yes, the organizations involved did consult their members and people whom they considered as "important Muslim voices", but most of these organizations have small memberships. African American Muslims, who, preferred to vote for Al Gore, were angry at the announcement and also felt alienated from the immigrant Muslims. One prominent

African American Muslim scholar angrily told me that the endorsement of Bush was abandonment of indigenous concerns and was a declaration that immigrant Muslims did not care for the opinion or the welfare of African American Muslims.

Younger Muslims, especially in the universities, wanted to vote for Nader and the Green Party. I could palpably feel their disenchantment, every time they said, "Our hearts are with Nader, but this time our vote is for Bush".

On hindsight, endorsing Bush has proved to be counter productive. We seem to have lesser access to policy makers now than we did during Clinton's beat. We have also generated a sense of resentment among Muslims that will take some time to simmer down. I hope in the future, American Muslim organizations will be more democratic and less presumptuous when making important decisions on behalf of all American Muslims.

Was there any other way out? Would we have been better off if one group had endorsed Bush and another endorsed Al Gore? We surely would not have been worse off, given the manner in which Bush has shrugged us off. The manner in which Bush has lately been cuddling up to the American Jewish lobby, which tried its best to defeat him, suggests that endorsements or block voting is no substitute for real political power.

Perhaps American Muslims are seeking easy shortcuts to power and influence in America. There is no such thing. We will have to dig in and do our homework the old fashioned way. Until we have serious access to, or significant control over the sources of power in American democracy, such as media, think tanks, all branches of the government and the corporate world, we will not be able to make a noticeable impact on American policies. Endorsing Bush was just one small step towards this. Perhaps we did not make a mistake in endorsing Bush, our mistake may be to expect too much from this singular act.

Muslims Should Not Support Federal Faith Based Programs

O ye who believe! If ye will aid (the cause of) Allah, He will aid you, and plant your feet firmly. – Qur'an 47: 7

President Bush's establishment of a White House office to facilitate the flow of federal funds to faith-based social initiatives engenders mixed responses.

It is a positive thing that government now recognizes the potential of spirituality to redress social ills such as poverty, drug addiction, alcoholism, and family crises. Indeed, it was the decline of spirituality and God consciousness that led to the emergence of social ills, particularly those connected with substance abuse and domestic abuse.

Bush has recognized the importance of spirituality and religious healing for social harmony. And in doing so, he has acknowledged that the existing programs have not been very successful in arresting the social decline of American society. For this and his bold demeanor in recognizing the problem-solving role of religion in society, President George W. Bush deserves to be applauded.

Having said that, as Muslims living in the U.S., we must be cautious about this initiative. Muslim organizations like Council on American and Islamic Relations (CAIR) and the American Muslim Council (AMC) have prematurely rushed to endorse this Bush initiative, while the Muslim Public Affairs Committee (MPAC) has shown guarded optimism. Groups like CAIR and AMC are probably laboring under the delusion that now Muslim organizations will be able to dip into the U.S. treasury to realize their goals. But these groups are sadly mistaken. By endorsing his initiative, they are working with crude interpretations of religion versus secularism and taking dangerous steps.

First of all, compared to the number of Christian organizations in the U.S., there are hardly any Muslim organizations in this country that provide social services which merit federal funding. There are some that deal with family counseling and with prisons, but the latter are usually geared toward *Dawah*, or proselytizing to Islam. If these organizations get money to do *Dawah* then it will really open the Pandora's box. Bush will give a few million dollars to some Islamic outfits and then start giving billions to the Christian Right. Imagine Pat Robertson and his outfit getting two billion dollars a year.

It's quite possible evangelical movements will use the federal funds for proselytizing as well as to establish themselves more firmly within the American government mechanism. Muslim leaders are now talking about establishing Islamic organizations for social service to benefit from this initiative. But if they are secretly dreaming of diverting these funds to other projects, then they are in for deep trouble.

If Pat Robertson or some other Christian group diverts some of this federal aid for other purposes, and they are caught, they will survive with little damage. But imagine if some Muslim outfit is caught using these funds to send medicines or relief to Palestine or Kashmir, then probably it will lead to a harassment of Muslim organizations of all kinds by the federal government. Even if no Muslim organization abuses this initiative, but is accused of doing so, it will be just as bad. We know that many Muslim relief organizations are already being harassed as of now.

Not only will faith based communities use these funds for proselytizing, they will also use them for discrimination. Can a Muslim drug addict go to a drug rehabilitation center where along with medication one has to believe that Jesus is God to find healing? Can he or she go to a Jewish or a Mormon establishment? Where will Muslim victims of social ills go to fight drug rehab, or treatment for alcohol addiction today? Also these religious establishments can refuse to offer services to people of other faiths.

He or she will probably have to go to the "secular establishments" which Muslim organizations oppose. But now these will be underfunded, and may not offer the best treatment.

Today Muslim social workers and therapists and psychologists are employed with these secular institutions. But these same workers will not be able to find jobs with Catholic, or Baptist organizations since they are legally allowed to discriminate while hiring and offering services.

Muslim organizations should not start chasing this so-called mixing of religion and politics in the U.S. It can be very dangerous.

The 1998 Religious Freedom initiative, another mixing of faith and government, has done nothing but engage in Islam bashing and work to evangelize Muslims in South Asia and Africa.

Imagine if these religious bodies were asked to provide policy input on immigration issues. They will stop immigration from Muslim countries. How far are Muslim organizations going to support the influx of religion into politics because they dislike secularism?

Some Muslim thinkers like to describe secularism as another religion. Fine, But if Muslim organizations are not opposed to the influence of Christianity, Judaism, Buddhism, Hinduism, and other religions on the Bush administration, then why should they be opposed to the influence of another faith – secularism, which will at least treat Muslims and Christians equally?

Muslims, especially when they are in a small minority, must be very wary of the influence of non-Islamic religions on governments that rule them. Even when Muslims impose Islamic principles, we must be careful about who gets to define what constitutes Islamic principles. Yes, secularism has lots of problems, because it tends to divest societies of their spiritual and even moral content. But replacing it with religious values that may not be compatible with ones own is not necessarily the best alternative.

Chapter 3
American Muslims
and American Foreign Policy

Islam and American Foreign Policy

*And did not God check one set of people by
means of another, the earth would indeed be
full of mischief: But God is full of bounty
to all the worlds.* – Qur'an 2: 251

In my research on American foreign policy towards contemporary Islamic resurgence – some call this phenomenon as Islamic
fundamentalism, some call it political Islam and yet others refer to it
as resurgent Islam – I identified interesting cleavages of opinion
between experts and practitioners. These cleavages suggest that the
U.S. does not have a monolithic view towards Islam and its policy can
change depending upon which element of the foreign policy community dominates.

There are three types of experts – policy entrepreneurs, those who
work for think tanks and other policy institutions, academics,
employed by universities, and practitioners, those who work for the
government. These three groups maintain different perspectives
and advance different policy positions towards Islam. The policy
entrepreneurs, exemplified by Dan Pipes and Judith Miller maintain
that fundamentalist Islam is inherently anti-West, anti-Israel and
anti-democratic. It is inevitably accompanied by terrorism and all its
adherents are, without exception, extremist. Therefore any and all
measures, even the compromise of America's democratic and liberal
values, must be employed to battle fundamentalist Islam and unstint-
ed support should be provided by the United States to all those in
combat with fundamentalist Islam. This hard line position makes no
distinction between those who wish to employ democratic means to

Islamize their society, such as Refa party of Turkey and the Muslim Brothers, and those who use militant and violent means to achieve the same end. Indeed the only moderate Muslims that Pipes has identified are Salman Rushdie and Taslima Nasreen. Most of the experts, interestingly, who hold this view are either influential journalists such as Steve Emerson and Mortimer Zuckermann or are employed with think tanks and are often friends of Israel.[2]

Academics on the other hand have a more nuanced and sophisticated understanding of the phenomenon. They are aware of the diversity in Islamic groups, in their character and their objectives. They do have a better grasp of the principles of Islam and its history and do not excessively employ the so called doctrine of *jihad* as the center piece of their analysis. Some of the famous academics who maintain that Islamic resurgence is a social movement, not necessarily opposed to America and certainly not undemocratic, are John Esposito, John Voll, Yvonne Haddad and Michael Hudson of Georgetown University, Edward Said, Richard Bulliet and Lisa Andersen of Columbia University, James Piscatori of the University of Wales and many more. These academics are seen as sympathetic to Islamic resurgence. John Esposito has argued that in principle the U.S. should not be opposed to Muslims applying the *Shariah* and John Antilles has advised the Congress to not fret if FIS comes to power in Algeria. The academics, most importantly, go to great pains to separate the moderates from the extremists and maintain that the violent prone elements of the Islamic resurgence are a small minority that is often radicalized by repressive and violent means employed by undemocratic and authoritarian and often illegitimate regimes that sadly prolifer-

---

2. For academic details see these articles by me: "Nice but Tough: A Framework for U.S. Foreign Policy in the Muslim World," *Brown Journal of World Affairs*, 9, 1 (Spring 2002), pp. 355-362. "U.S. Foreign Policy and Political Islam: Interests, Ideas and Ideology", *Security Dialogue*, 29, 4, (Dec. 1998), pp. 449.462. "Policy Entrepreneurs: The Third Dimension of American Foreign Policy Culture," *Middle East Policy*, (September 1997), pp. 140-154. "The Ethic of Resentment: A Nietzschean Analysis of Islam and the West, " *Middle East Affairs*, (Spring 1999), pp. 161-173. "Imagining the Threat of (Fundamentalist) Islam", *Middle East Affairs* (Fall 1999), pp. 175-185.

ate the Muslim horizon. They advise the U.S. to negotiate and even work with Islamists where they do not challenge American interests directly.

The practitioners have a well-articulated policy that sounds very much like a conservative version of the academics' recommendations. However their actions often belie their policy rhetoric. The U.S. government is up-front in stating that it has no quarrel with Islam and that it recognizes Islam as one of the great religions and as a great   civilizing influence in history. They also assert that they are not in principle opposed to Islamization. However when it comes to implementation the government leaves a lot to be desired. Its recent conduct when Israel bombed Lebanon is to say the least unbecoming of a self proclaimed champion of democracy and freedom and one that lays claim to world leadership. Its bombings of Sudan and Afghanistan not to mention its continuing sanctions over Iraq suggest that the administration has yet to reduce the gap between rhetoric and action.

American Muslims can and should intervene in the policy process. They can do so by adopting a three-pronged strategy. One, cooperate with the administration where there are common interests. The recent cooperation between Muslim groups and the United States in providing aid and assistance to Kosova is a great beginning and must be exploited. American Muslims must understand that there are legitimate American interests and when American interests clash with the interests of their "former homelands" they must be with America, their "new homeland". Otherwise they will be seen and labeled as traitors, untrustworthy. American Muslims must realize that they cannot push two agendas, nationalism and Islam at the same time. In the interest of Islam they must gainsay nationalism (a form of tribalism which has no room in Islam any way).

Two, American Muslims must work with the academics and seek in every possible way to strengthen them so that they can have greater influence in policy shaping. And finally, Muslim researchers and activists must expose the "special interests" that the policy entrepreneurs are pushing. There is no point in constantly labeling them as enemies of Islam. What is important is to show how the policies they recommend are not in the long-term interests of the U.S.. That will marginalize them. It is time we reduced the decibel level of anti-West, anti-U.S. rhetoric and focused on the more serious and important task of reshaping Western attitudes, perceptions and policies through research and hard work.

Islam, Religious Freedom and U.S. Foreign Policy

Let there be no compulsion in religion.
– Qur'an 2: 256

We have bestowed dignity on the children of Adam.
– Qur'an 17: 70

The State Department now regularly consults American Muslims on matters relating to Islam and the Muslim World. One of its initiatives was a one day conference on "Islam and Religious Freedom", held at Meridian House in Washington, DC on November 14, 2000.

The purpose of the conference was soliciting Muslim perspectives on the new report on International Religious Freedom that it was about to publish. In this conference, the State Department learned that in the eyes of Muslims, this latest U.S. initiative is perceived as a governmental attempt to assist Christian missionaries overseas.

By passing the International Religious Freedom's Act in 1998, the Congress has mandated the State Department to furnish annual reports on the state of religious freedom in every country on the planet. The ostensible purpose of this exercise is to advance religious freedom, a value that the State Department now describes as a "core objective" of American foreign policy. The norms and principles of religious freedom that guide this report are based on Articles 18, 19 of the International Covenant on Civil and Political Rights (ICCPR) and article 18 of the Universal Declaration of Human Rights (UDHR), which argue that freedom of religion is an inalienable human right.

No one could possibly argue with the wisdom and universal validity of these principles. The U.S. government truly deserves accolades for making religious freedom a core objective of its foreign policy. Nevertheless, there is something highly suspicious about this report and it becomes quite evident on closer examination. Since 1977 the State Department has been submitting to the U.S. Congress an annual report on human rights in every country. That report is also guided by ICCPR and UDHR and therefore does cover the issue of religious freedoms in every country. Then what is the need for this additional instrument? The answer is simple. This report covers issues that interest those who are seeking to proselytize people to Christianity in Asia and Africa, the heartlands of Islam. The report is designed to identify legal and customary barriers to change of faith so that the U.S. government can apply pressure to eliminate them.

Consider this specific congressional requirement; the report is required to keep track of every minor that is forcibly converted in all countries of the world. Conversion of minors? According to article 18 of the ICCPR parents and guardians have the right to bring their children up according to whatever religion they wish. In other words, children do not have a right to religious freedom. Parents enjoy the privilege of imparting religious education to their offspring without state intervention. This puzzling Congressional requirement can only be understood if one connects it to a curious domestic problem involving marriages between Muslim immigrant men and non-Muslim American women. In the event of a divorce, Islamic law usually gives custody to the father after they reach a certain age and under the American judicial system, custody of the children is usually given to the mother. After losing custody battles in America, Muslim men sometimes run away home with their kids to bring them up as Muslims fearing their ex-wife would bring them up Christian.

There are over 200 such pending cases in the U.S. at the moment and Christian missionaries in the U.S. have been deeply agitated by this phenomenon. The U.S. Congress is now mandating the State Department to track these children fearing that they will be brought up Muslim. While the U.S. may see this as defending the right of

American born kids to grow up Christian, Muslims see this as a
governmental interference, in some cases as foreign intervention with
the right of a parent (in this case a father) to bring up his kids as
Muslims. This is just one of the many indicators in the report which
suggest that the State Department has been recruited for missionary
purposes. The report, in each case has only focused on barriers to
Christianity. Meanwhile, the U.S. government has paid little attention
and sometimes completely ignoring, how other religious minorities
such as Muslims in India, South Africa, Europe and the U.S.,
Buddhists in China, Hindus in the Middle East, Bangladesh and
Pakistan suffer religious and political discrimination.

American Muslims are deeply concerned about the lack of political and religious freedoms in the Middle East and Asia. They believe
that Muslims themselves are the biggest victims of oppression and
tyranny in the Muslim World. They are keen to work with the U.S.
and international human rights institutions to remedy the situation.
But first, they insist instruments like the report on international religious freedoms must be fair, balanced and objective. Taking sides
overtly in the missionary market place will not only hurt the cause of
religious tolerance, but also elicit negative responses that may further
jeopardize religious minorities already in danger.

America's Middle East Policy: Is There Room for Balance?

*... make peace between them with justice, and be fair:
For Allah loves those who are fair (and just).*
– Qur'an 49: 9

The entire world saw Muhammad Aldurra, a 12-year-old
Palestinian boy shot to pieces by the Israeli army. He was just
one of the many Palestinian children killed or injured in Al-Aqsa
intifada. What the world did not see was President Clinton mourning
the death of this child, who died without freedom. What the world did
not see was a promise from an American President that this would
never happen again.

The U.S. plays a double role in the Arab-Israeli conflict as Israel's staunchest ally and as a broker of peace. As a broker of peace, its security guarantee to Israel is designed to enable Israel to take risks for peace. For the Palestinians, the U.S. has promised a homeland and financial assistance for development if they took all the necessary steps toward peace. These steps include, cessation of armed struggle against Israel and acceptance of Israel as a sovereign nation.

After nearly a decade of peace talks the Palestinians have got nothing but a fresh taste of Israeli brutality. Who is to blame for this nothingness and hopelessness?

It is the American policy that is singularly responsible for the failure of peace in the Middle East. Every time talks fail, Americans blame the Palestinians and Arafat. And when the Palestinians threatened to take unilateral steps such as a declaration of statehood, the U.S. Congress passed a bill not only promising to deny recognition but also threatening to cut aid necessary for nation building. But when Israelis back away, the U.S. merely provides more guarantees. And when Israelis use egregious and excessive force, killing children and civilians, Americans hedge about the blame and provide damage control in international forums. This policy of unlimited and uncritical support of Israel only enhances its arrogance and reckless disregard for Palestinian lives.

Israeli existence is dependent on an American security guarantee and it has prospered from American generosity. Even a suggestion that the U.S. would cut aid or reduce support could make Israel more willing to make peace and less inclined to use brutal force. Enemies of peace like Ariel Sharon can become persona nongrata over night if Americans condemn them publicly. Plus American willingness to discipline Israel would build more confidence in the Palestinians and they would be willing to trust the U.S. and make more sacrifices for peace.

Not only is American policy one sided but also its representatives. American Jews are actively included at every level in policy making. For example the important people in Clinton's Middle East team, Martin Indyk (U.S. Ambassador to Israel) and Dennis Ross (U.S.

Special Envoy) were both Jewish Americans. Indyk is in fact a former lobbyist for a pro-Israel PAC. But Arab Americans are never included and rarely consulted in policy making. For Arabs and Palestinians, this symbolizes American one sidedness and an unwillingness to trust and include them.

In order that there be peace, it is not sufficient that Israel alone get what it wants. America will have to promise something to the Palestinians too. It can begin by trying to be fair and evenhanded. In the after math of September 11, President Bush acknowledged the need for a Palestinian State. But for over a year, the Bush administration has maintained a handoff approach to the Middle East crisis allowing violence to rage and the gains made by the peace process diminish rapidly. Peace can only come to the region if the U.S., which sustains the military imbalance in the region, takes firm and fair steps to initiate and maintain a negotiated outcome.

U.S. Foreign Policy in the Middle East: A Barrier to Democracy?

So He hath put as a consequence hypocrisy into their hearts, (to last) till the Day, whereon they shall meet Him: because they broke their covenant with God, and because they lied (again and again). – Qur'an 9: 97

The catastrophic attacks on the World Trade Center and the Pentagon have raised several questions about Islam and militant Muslims. The chief among them are, why are some Muslims so angry at the U.S. that they would perpetrate such an inhuman act?

There are several theories being advanced by various commentators explaining why militant Muslims hate the United States. The silliest of them is the one that the Bush administration and the conservative elements in America entertain. They insist that Muslim militants hate America because they hate American values of freedom and democracy. Nothing can be further from the truth. Indeed most of us Muslims are great admirers of self-determination, pluralism and freedom and insist that these values are not only consistent with Islam but were the bedrock of the glorious Islamic civilization. We always point to the diversity, tolerance and harmony at the peak of Islamic civilization to substantiate their claims.

As Islamic awareness increases in postcolonial Muslim societies and Islamic activists try to rebuild their civilization they find that an economically motivated alliance between secular authoritarian regimes in the Muslim world and the West, in particular the U.S., is the biggest barrier to freedom, democracy and self determination. Algeria, Saudi Arabia, Bahrain, Kuwait are just a few examples of states where non-democratic regimes thrive and repress popular movements with U.S. support. The U.S. government finds it more convenient to dominate the region by negotiating terms with a handful of elite rather than coming to terms with the region's public opinion, if democracy were to take root in the Middle East.

In 1953 a CIA coup replaced the democratic government of Muhammed Mossadeq in Iran with a monarchy so that Iran could become a client serving U.S. interests in the Middle East. In Algeria the West financed and legitimized a military coup that prevented Islamists from coming to power after winning an election. The U.S. remains a close ally and even defender of nearly all the monarchies in the region. The Kings of Saudi Arabia and Jordan are crucial to U.S. interests in the region.

Since the Taliban took over in Afghanistan the American establishment has railed about its human rights record and treatment of women, but nothing is said about Saudi Arabia, which is not very different from Afghanistan on these very issues.

There is also a false notion circulating that Islam and democracy are incompatible. Today nearly 650 million Muslims live in democratic societies (Turkey, Bangladesh, India, Indonesia, Iran, Europe, North America, Malaysia, Australia). As of now there are two Muslim nations that have women heads of state – Indonesia and Bangladesh. Pakistan and Turkey have had women leaders in the past. The U.S. has not had one in over 220 years! (Interestingly even the present chief of Amnesty International is a Muslim woman).

It is not a hatred of democracy and freedom but the desire for one that has made many Muslims angry at the U.S. whom they blame for the perpetuation of undemocratic polities in their world. Surely there are some Muslims who argue that democracy like everything Western is UnIslamic. Fortunately such misguided people are few and have very little influence in the Muslim World.

The utter lack of peaceful channels for protest and dissent in the entire Arab world has slowly radicalized most moderate Islamic oppositions. The use of brutal force by secular regimes has further incited reactionary violence from Islamic militias. Many Muslims from this part of the world believe that the U.S. is hypocritical about its claim that it values democracy. They also think that it is inherently opposed to democracy in the Muslim world and must share the blame for the repression and authoritarianism perpetrated by its allies.

The mounting frustration at their inability to bring change in their own world has led many Muslims to take the militant route and now they are zeroing in on the U.S., who in their opinion is the biggest barrier to political freedom.

Does this mean that angry Muslims are allowed to perpetrate collateral damages that include over 3000 innocent Americans? Certainly not. The purpose of this article is not to condone what happened on September 11. What happened was horrible, inhuman and unIslamic.

But reflection over Muslim grievances can help us understand how even devout people can be driven to commit themselves to terror. Systematic repression dispossesses people of their humanity, inciting them to commit inhuman acts.

Americans must take these grievances seriously and address them in good faith and that, in my opinion, is the best way to fight resentment, anger and the resulting violence.

Kosova: A Watershed in U.S. – Islamic Relations

Of the good that they (Christians and Jews) do, nothing will be rejected of them; for God knoweth well those that do right. – Qur'an 3:115

The NATO campaign against Serbia was a major step toward the restoration of international law and the respect for human and minority rights globally. The campaign, at the time, also resuscitated the U.S. image as a superpower committed to global security and welfare. But the most remarkable, and perhaps unintended, consequence of NATO's humanitarian mission in Kosova was the re-evaluation of the United States by Muslims in the West as well as in the Muslim world. In the aftermath of September 11 and U.S. attack on Afghanistan it is important for both the U.S. and Muslims in general to recall the good will that was generated by U.S. actions on behalf of the Kosovars.

For too long Muslims at all levels, from intellectuals to the man in the street, had been laboring under the impression that the sole purpose of U.S. foreign policy is to undermine the growth of Islam and the welfare of Muslims everywhere. The unwavering U.S. commitment to Israel, the implacable U.S. sanctions against Iraq even after acknowledging the great suffering of innocent Iraqis, and particularly Iraqi children, and unceasing U.S. opposition to the Islamic regime in Iran, are only among some of the many instances frequently cited by Muslims as evidence of a continuing American crusade against Islam.

Nevertheless, there are Muslim intellectuals who consider the "clash of civilizations" thesis as nonsense and who have tried to convince their co-religionists that while the pursuit of American national and cultural interests may sometimes clash with the strategic and cultural interests of Muslims, the U.S. in fact is a self-centered nation in search of global self-actualization, and not of excuses for Islam-bashing. In support of this argument, Muslim moderates point to American relations with Saudi Arabia and its fellow Gulf Cooperation Council member nations and, above all, the relative freedom and security in which over six million Muslims live, thrive, prosper and propagate Islam in America, as concrete evidence that the U.S. is not anti-Islam. But until now, these arguments were easily dismissed by the critics of the U.S. as necessary to maintain its oil supplies and to sustain a charade of domestic freedom and democracy.

The centrality and utterly indispensable role of the U.S. in the Kosova affair had for the first time made more open-minded Muslims, particularly those residing in the U.S., re-examine the popular image of the U.S. as the great Satan and enemy of Islam. The protracted nature of the U.S. diplomatic and military effort and the thoroughgoing coverage the U.S. media provided of the suffering of Muslims in Kosova had gradually restored some of the long-missing Muslim confidence in American media.

Importantly, the public expressions of pain and agony by American leaders over the carnage in Kosova suddenly gave American leaders a new humanistic dimension. From being global tormentors of Islam they became, almost overnight, sympathetic allies of Muslims, sharing their pain and struggling with them in a common, humanitarian cause.

The image of American planes and missiles hitting Muslim targets in Libya, in Iraq, in Sudan and Afghanistan had become so common-place that Muslims easily came to the conclusion that U.S. concern for human rights and democracy is just hypocrisy and doublespeak. While U.S. leaders lament the plight of Christians in Sudan and Indonesia and Jews in Iran, they have shown little concern for the plight of the Palestinians, Kashmiris or the Chechens.

Similarly, while Americans have for decades opposed the Islamic regimes in Iran and Sudan for their authoritarianism, the U.S. has allowed secular fundamentalists to use equally undemocratic methods to prevent Islamists from coming to power democratically in Algeria or to keep increasingly unpopular secularists illegitimately in power in Turkey.

But the sight of American pilots repeatedly sent into harm's way to protect Muslims and bomb the Serbian Christian soldiers that menaced them shattered stereotypes. In fact, it seemed so unbelievable that some diehard America haters continue to advance extremely complex and convoluted conspiracy theories about how the rescue of Kosova is just another diabolic American scheme against Islam. But for many Muslims it has been an eye-opener.

Muslims then were willing to accept the stated objectives of American leaders. The American efforts in Bosnia, followed by American support for peace in the Middle East despite the obvious disdain of Israeli leaders, and now the Kosova affair have significantly enhanced the credibility of American concerns for peace, democracy and human rights in the minds of Muslims, especially among those who actually live in the West and can observe the American people as well as their government at first hand.

The U.S. administration must be applauded for the manner in which it cooperated with American Muslims in organizing relief work and in helping the refugees. While there are more than 10,000 Muslims in the U.S. military, this was the first time that American Muslims felt that they were working with the U.S. in pursuit of a common goal. And, more significantly, this was also the first time that both parties fully trusted and cooperated with each other.

Indeed, this U.S. gesture of trust has gone a long way in making American Muslims feel at home and proud of being Americans. In several discussion groups on the Internet, at various community seminars and in question-and-answer sessions after public lectures, this new mood was palpable.

As a result of this singular event, American Muslims were increasingly re-imagining the U.S. and its global leadership. All the pro-U.S. arguments advanced by moderate Muslim intellectuals in the past were now getting more attention. The hawks were sulking and the doves were smiling. While one cannot expect an overnight "paradigm change" in the outlook of most Muslims toward the U.S., its inspiring response to the tragic episode of Kosova had provided a good foundation stone for a new beginning in cultural and civilizational bridge building.

Chapter 4

American Muslims and American Society

The Emerging Challenge of Postmodernity

And they have no knowledge of it;
they do not follow anything but conjecture,
and surely conjecture does not avail against
the truth at all. – Qur'an 53: 28

For over three hundred years, Islam has faced the challenge of European enlightenment and modernity. Compared to other religions, Islam has performed formidably. While the significance of nearly all religions has receded to the "private domain" or even into vestigial customs and occasional rituals, Islam has experienced a major resurgence in the twentieth century. The scars of modernity, however, are easy to see on the face of the Muslim World.

Secularism and Nationalism, two of modernity's strong manifestations are now well entrenched in many parts of the Muslim World. Ideologies emerging from the conditions of modernity such as Marxism and Liberalism continue to compete with Islam in trying to shape Muslim societies. Even Muslim intellectuals who seek scholarly acceptance are compelled to succumb to modernist discourses, thereby furthering the agenda of modernity at the expense of Islam.

Islam and modernity, one must remember, are not necessarily antithetical. Indeed one could argue that the genesis of enlightenment and modernity could be found in thriving medieval Islamic civilization. However modernity has taken many wrong turns in the last century by corrupting its own foundational principles. The value of "freedom," understood by Kant as freedom to do good, is now understood as freedom to do anything. Reason has been displaced by instrumental reason. Knowledge has become the servant of power.

Wisdom has been replaced by public opinion. Even as Muslims enjoy the fruits of modernity, Islam continues to struggle against the dark side of modernity.

The emergence of large Muslim populations in the West, particularly in America, has opened a new chapter in the dialogue between Islam and modernity. However, even before the Muslim-Modernity encounter could reach a resolution, a new challenge emerged – postmodernity.

The postmodern challenge manifests itself in two separate but equally devastating forms. One is cultural and the other is philosophical (epistemological). On the cultural front, postmodern manifestations in the form of new social movements (e.g., art forms, politics or lifestyles) have joyously disrupted the neat order of things that reason had established in the heyday of modernity. On the epistemological front, postmodern incursions have subverted not only the foundations of truth, but also the possibility of ever establishing any truth claims.

Suddenly perversion is an alternate lifestyle. God-consciousness, long understood as enlightenment, is now bigotry and an indicator of social underdevelopment. There is no absolute Truth only contingent truths. Morality is reduced to conventions that work and justice is an option that enjoys political support. The self is no more the mystical domain where the spiritual and mundane merge. Life is no more the discovery and the perfection of that self. Today self is something you buy of a shelf. Life is a careful compilation and continuous renovation of that self. Philosophy and revelation are no more the maps for self-discovery. They have been displaced by catalogues, e-stores and home-shopping networks. Postmodern intrusions have systematically subverted and undermined every pillar of modern culture, turning it on its head and making it a parody of itself.

If the cultural assault of postmodernism is devastating, than its epistemological assault cannot be described as anything but as "writing the epitaph of modernity". While modernity decenterred God and in its place crowned reason as the sovereign authority that alone determined the legitimacy of truth claims, postmodernity has chosen to dethrone not only reason but the very notion of authority and the very idea of truth.

How then in the postmodern vision will the project of civilization survive or progress? The answer is more than startling. All projects are illegitimate because they undermine competing projects and because it is power, not any intrinsic worth, that determines which project becomes the civilizational project. Progress is a myth. Without God, without reason, without a worldview, how do we live? The postmodern answer is let life itself find the way. So just live, "just do it" and life will lead you to life.

The prophets of postmodernity and their cohort have little to offer. Foucault says power is god. Derrida says dance to the sound as human civilization is deconstructed – god by god and idea by idea. Rorty says let life be guided by success, it does not matter if there is no intrinsic good in life or success. Habermas, dreams of a special reason -- communicative rationality – that will be more reasonable than reason itself. He places the future of the self in understanding the other, while the other continues to plot the annihilation of the self.

This crisis of Truth can be comforting to none. The decline of the spiritual and moral dimensions of Western society increasingly suggest that a society which is gradually relinquishing the quest for truth may eventually have nothing to pursue. Freedom for Freedom's sake has never sustained a civilization. It does not promise to make amends in the future either. Freedoms based on widely held truths have in the past, generated great civilizations but never without essential foundations.

As a contemporary Islamic philosopher, living in the dusk of modernity and in the heart of the West, deeply nostalgic for a divine-ly ordained order of things that is consistent with reason and justice, full of compassion and mercy, I am fascinated by the systematic deconstruction of modernity by the very forces it engendered and unleashed upon itself. The normative structure of boundless freedom and a culture of irreverence that modernity has deliberately fostered to subvert God has now turned upon its creator.

Skepticism based on the assumed infallibility and universal sovereignty of reason was the constitutive character of modernity. It was designed to eliminate faith and re-channel Man's inherent compulsion to submit and worship. New Gods and new traditions were invented, new prophets were proclaimed and new heavens were imagined. But religion has not only survived the five hundred year assault on God and his messages, but has returned with an increased fervor that baffles the postmodern being.

The postmodern being, whose heart without faith is empty and mind without reason is immature, can destroy the fragile foundations of modernity and ridicule the memories of tradition but can neither comprehend nor deal with the resurgence of faith. Those waging a losing battle for modernity against postmodernity reject the resurgence of faith as a return to backward premodernity. Their short-sightedness precludes them from imagining the resurgence of faith not as a return but as a leap forward.

For those who were always with God and comfortable with reason, in the tradition of Al Ghazali, Ibn Khaldun and Ibn Rushd, the resurgence of religion is merely the continuation of the divine way. Islam never succumbed either to modernity nor is losing out to postmodernity. Islam's decline was geopolitical and economic, never epistemological. The entire musical chairs of authority, God, Reason, Conventions, Text, and Nothing, is Western and limited to those societies who have succumbed to the forces of modernism completely.

Islam was from the beginning comfortable with reason, recognizing its immense potential and necessity but also remaining acutely cognizant of its limitation. The Al Ghazali-Ibn Rushd debate on the nature of causality is an excellent chronicle of Islam's position on reason. Islam simultaneously recognized the absoluteness of Truth as well as the relativity of truth claims. For over 1400 years Muslims have believed in one *Shariah* but recognized more than four different, competing and even contradictory articulations of this *Shariah* (*madhahib*).

Islam has survived the experiment called modernity and will survive the bonfire (postmodernity) that is threatening to burn down the lab along with the experiment. There is sufficient play in terms of epistemological pluralism, whether it is recognition of the validity of different legal opinions based on different contexts or time or based on different discursive epistemes such as *burhan* – illumination, *jadal* -- dialectics, and *khatabath* – rhetoric, that will allow Islam to negotiate postmodernity's epistemological rampage.

Muslims in America will have to confront the challenge of post-modernity. It will force them to expand their conceptions of what constitutes a family, become open to subversive educational texts that will deny not only absolute truths based on revelation but also truths based on reason and science. Most importantly, the postmodern atmosphere will try to inculcate a feeling of guilt among Muslims for harboring faith in their hearts. Its most brutal assault will be in the form of social derision and contempt for Islamic values for not extending a theological welcome to the gay lifestyle. The feminist attacks on Islam and its influence on how Islam is perceived has set the framework for future assaults on Islam.

How Islam faces the challenge of postmodernity will depend not only on how American Muslims interpret and practice Islam but how they deal with the strategic demands of such an encounter. American Muslims must prepare themselves to distinguish between the principles of Islam and the accumulated cultural practices in the Muslim World (many acquired from Pre-Islamic days or from the West under colonial rule).They must interpret the former with compassion and critique the latter rigorously.

Islam and Race Relations in America

And of His signs is the creation
of the heavens and the earth, and the difference
of your languages and colors. – Qur'an 30: 22

Had Allah willed He could have made you
one community? But that He may try you by
that which He hath given you (He hath made
you as ye are). So vie one with another in
good works. – Qur'an 5: 48

With a history of slavery, racial discrimination and intolerance, America has had more than its share of social divisions and internal discord. Needless to say, it still remains the best example of tolerance and pluralism that has been achieved in the modern world. While it was the white American who practiced racism, it was also white Americans who took up arms to end racism – whether it be through religious violence, abolitionists, or through a civil war. Nowhere in the world, do racial or any other minorities enjoy as much freedom or come so close to operational equality as do African-Americans or Hispanics in the U.S.A. In many Muslim states, discrimination based on ethnicity is widespread. In some of these states, even salaries are based on ethnicity rather than experience or qualifications.

The crux of the argument is simple. For all its deficiencies in eliminating discrimination, America is found lacking only in comparison to its own ideals and not with respect to any real society anywhere on the planet. Therefore, I am suggesting to all Muslims, of every race and ethnicity, to recognize the "good thing" they have here in America and do something about making it better, or at least to try and arrest its decline. Even after the decline in the general standards of civil rights protection as a result of Attorney General Ashcroft's and President Bush's war on terrorism, America remains an incredibly free and tolerant society.

This appeal to American Muslims to contribute to improving race relations in America is not solely based on the fact that they have benefited from it, but on a sound premise that they are in an advantageous position to facilitate it. Before I get into articulating the role that American Muslims can play to improve race (un)relations, it would be useful to take a stock of the situation. For below the general nationalistic fervor, there are three major social undercurrents flowing in America. They are, racism, ethnicity and religiosity.

In conditions when flag waving is not the most important preoccupation of the populace at large, as it was during the World Wars, the Cold War, and most recently during the televised Gulf War, these undercurrents begin to influence the socio-political discourse of the country. The end of the Cold War has turned the country inside out. While formerly it was externally focused on geopolitics, on keeping a close eye on the oil wells, on counting of guns and modern catapults, and on trying to peep over the iron curtain, it now has become internally focused. It is now more concerned with health care, crime, taxes, and on the life and times of former football greats.

After years of external orientation and of believing the autobiographical discourse (propaganda) of a society based on freedom and equality of opportunity, Americans are aghast and a tad bit irritated with the America that is less than what they believed it to be. All the divisions, the fault lines, and the oversights in public policy are slowly coming into focus as Americans take a long look at the America that came out victorious in the long and tedious, expensive and dangerous cold war. The irritated reaction, manifest in the pungent rhetoric on the airways, or even in Congress, is doing more to aggravate the deficiencies than to address them constructively.

It is in this atmosphere of social tension and vitriolic discourse that Muslims of America, who have benefited from the generosity and even tolerance of this great country, should pay their dues when it needs it most. Muslims in America number anywhere around six million, according to a Congressional Quarterly Researcher report. This same report, (April 1993) also suggests that over 40%, of them are non-immigrant Americans. While there is no census data available to make scientific arguments as to the racial or ethnic makeup of Muslims, enough anecdotal evidence is available to argue that American Muslims include substantial numbers from both white and black races. Indeed, in some Muslim congregations in Northern Virginia, Caucasians as well as African Americans act as Imams. Muslims who follow their religion are able to transcend racial boundaries. It may be a rare sight to see a Caucasian member of an African American church, but to see a white offer *namaaz* (Muslim prayer) behind a black Imam, and vice versa is commonplace in mosques everywhere.

Christianity, Islam's older cousin, has similar universal claims. However, its execution in America has been far from impeccable.

There are white churches and there are black churches. At one time this segregation was formal. Now it is informal, habitual and perhaps even ideological. There is a White Jesus (peace and blessings be upon him) and a Black Jesus (pbuh too). Christianity in America, rather than transcending and eliminating racial discrimination and segregation, has succumbed to the evils of color intolerance.

Fortunately, Muslims have so far successfully resisted this evil. Again many would disagree with this, but even the most intransigent of anti-Islamicists would agree that racial discrimination was never institutionalized in Islamic history. They will also agree that Prophet Mohammed (pbuh) has never been ahistorically appropriated by any racial or ethnic group.

We may recall that Malcolm X, one of the most militant of black racist leaders, completely turned a new leaf after his pilgrimage to Makkah. He was struck by the colorblind nature of Islam. On his return to America his actions changed and his political pronouncements are evidence to this transformation. This argument is certainly not an attempt to market Islam as the solution to racial discord in America. It is an attempt to identify a widening window in American society that is colorblind. A large group of Americans, who adhere to a set of values which has no room whatsoever for racial considerations, is gradually emerging as Islam settles in the States. And it is this multiracial group that can facilitate dialogue and action to bring the two races together. It is American Muslims who can and should act as mediators.

American Muslims are now in a position to introduce a third dimension into the race equation, which can both mediate as well as demonstrate. American Muslims already manifest racial harmony in Mosques, in community center related activities and even in inter-racial marriages. There are over 1500 Islamic Centers in the USA and most of them are exemplary centers of racial harmony. The only place where this is missing is in the centers of the Nation of Islam and the reasons for such a state is self-evident. But Muslims seem to keep this to themselves. And it is here that they can play a role by introducing the third dimension in America's race relations by opening up their communities to America.

By becoming more visible and more prominent in America, American Muslims can show that yes, indeed, communities and individuals once suffering from racial prejudice can overcome them. As Nietzsche says, it is the overcoming of the self, rather than struggling to overcome the other, which is the greatest virtue of all. They should invite non-Muslim Black and White neighbors to their community functions and open their Mosques and centers for visitation. Muslims should include the subject of race relations in their discourse, on community television programs, and in their magazines and journals. Some Muslims themselves feel that they are victims of discrimination and stereotyping. But by participating in America's prominent struggles, they cannot only make themselves more at home, but also be accepted through a more positive contribution to its society. It is only by embracing America's problems will they be more acceptable to America. And in my opinion the best way to do that is through offering a third point of view in American race relations through demonstration as well as participation. Every ordinary Muslim today becomes an ambassador of Islam, either by choice or in defense. We are always explaining how *jihad* is not a holy war, and how every one of us is not a cousin of Saddam Hussein and how like ordinary humans, we Muslims too have a heart and a soul. To this burden of being a Muslim, I would like to add the onerous duty of carrying a message, not just in words but in deeds, of racial harmony. We have benefited from the tolerance and plenitude of this society, it is only fitting that we should pay our dues.

Tocqueville in his Democracy in America made some interesting observations that are germane to the discussion here. He remarked that while in the South, laws were employed to maintain a distance between the Black and White races. In the North, informal customs had emerged which performed the same task. Whether through institutionalized or informal practices, the two races have maintained a distance between them. The lesson one learns from Tocqueville is that it is not laws that change people. We need something more than legislation to bring about racial harmony in America. Perhaps

Tocqueville himself has an answer. He argued that perhaps the reason why Democracy has prevailed at all levels in America is due to the hands-on experience that Americans had with democratic practices. He suggested that through local institutions, Americans were practicing democracy even before they became a nation. It is this hands-on experience of racial harmony that is absent in America. It is this lacuna in the American experience that Islam and American Muslims can fill. American Muslims can bring their experience with racial harmony, an experience that was not precipitated by laws or by custom but by a recognition and internalization of the sense of equality between races in the eyes of God. If the American Muslims can bring this experience with racial harmony to America, it will be easily their greatest contribution to America and American democracy.

America and the Crisis of Integrity

O ye who believe! Betray not Allah and His messenger, nor knowingly betray your trusts. – Qur'an 8: 27

The shadow of September 11 and the various crises such as Enron and the Middle East that have followed it have obscured an important aspect of the contemporary American condition. America today is experiencing a crisis of integrity. The common denominator that links the Enron fiasco, the crisis in the Catholic Church, the failure of U.S. foreign policy in the Middle East, the patriotism of media, the derailment of the war on terror and the downward spiral of civil rights protection in the U.S. is the steady compromise of moral integrity in American society.

The Enron fiasco highlighted two dangerous trends. The mismanagement of Enron's finances stemmed from a combination of greed and a callous disregard for law. In pursuit of higher profits, Enron's executives not only tried to cut corners but also attempted successfully to undermine the integrity of public and private watchdog agencies. Through campaign finance and access to decision making in the White House, former Enron CEO Kenneth Lay was able to influence the control of federal regulatory agency. By using the carrot of additional business through consultation, Enron corrupted Arthur Anderson, whose job as its accountant firm was to check for the very violations of securities and trade regulations that it facilitated to conceal. In the case of Enron both the Federal government and Arthur Anderson violated their trusts.

The sex scandal in the Catholic Church exposes the moral frailty of the spiritual and the religious sphere of American society. The Catholic Church is not only the biggest religious institution in America it is also the biggest institution outside the Federal government. The sex scandal not only shows that over a thousand of its officials violated the ethics of their community, violated the trust and person of their wards but also committed deplorable crimes against society by preying on the most vulnerable, young and innocent members of society. The church scandal has an equivalent of Arthur Anderson in the person of Cardinal Law. Like Arthur Anderson, Cardinal Law too violated his most important duty, to protect those who trust in him. His attempts to conceal crime and not take any action to prevent future occurrence of abuse constitute an enormous breach of integrity. Coming from a Cardinal, one of the highest spiritual ranks in our society, such deliberate dereliction of duty defies description.

The practice of violating ethics to protect the institutions created to advance the very same ethics can also be detected in the actions of the U.S. government in its response to September 11. The most important objective of the U.S. government is to protect and realize the principles enshrined in the U.S. constitution. Unfortunately to defend democracy and freedom, the present government has decided to violate many of the principles and values that constitute democracy and freedom. The new laws, as in the Patriot act, designed to preempt terrorism and prosecute alleged terrorists clearly subvert several articles of the bill of rights that protect the rights to due process, fair and speedy trials and protect citizens from illegal searches and seizures. The Patriot act in targeting terrorists also ends up targeting the bill of rights.

Another instance where the present government is skirting civil rights responsibilities is with regards to those who were captured in Afghanistan. The government is holding these prisoners as detainees in Guantanamo Bay, Cuba to remain outside the jurisdiction of American courts. If these prisoners were on American soil, American courts could order that their rights be protected. Moreover the administration has decided not to fulfill all the requirements stipulated by Geneva conventions and International Law on POWs and is doing so by refusing to acknowledge them as prisoners of war. The international community, particularly European media and governments, has strongly criticized the condition of these prisoners.

U.S. policies in the aftermath of September 11 have subverted and compromised the inalienability of democratic and human rights by making them seem like luxuries that can be afforded only under secure conditions. The U.S. as the world's most prominent democracy is sending a wrong signal to the rest of the world. It is suggesting that in moments of crisis and insecurity even the most powerful of states cannot afford to protect democracy, human rights and international laws. Most other nations are far more insecure and often in crisis, how can we then demand that they adhere to international norms and protect civil and political rights of their citizens?

In a democracy the role of the media is to hold the government accountable for its actions and policies. But after September 11 one increasingly finds reporters and anchormen succumbing to misguided patriotism. Wearing of flags on the suit lapels seems to have become standard uniform for many. In their rush to demonstrate their patriotism and nationalism the media has abdicated its primary responsibility and has become reluctant to challenge or criticize the President and his administration on its conduct of the war on terror and for its role in the Enron fiasco and for the declining human rights standards. The only exception to the rule is when any move by the President or the administration threatens Israeli interests. Then no one is spared. I wish our media would protect American interests with the same zeal that it protects Israeli interests.

Whether it is the private sector, or the public sector or the realm of religion and spirituality, prominent American institutions have recently shown a marked proclivity to compromising of values. The failure of these sections of American society is exaggerated by the failure of the American media that too has allowed September 11 to undermine its own integrity. Surely it is important that we meet all challenges; but we should not repeat the mistake made by Cardinal Law who in his earnestness to protect the Catholic Church, forgot to protect Catholics and Catholic values. We must protect America, and we must also not forget to protect our normative values.

As American Muslims we can probably have a greater impact on American society by intervening as a normative agent of change rather than a political actor. It sounds like day dreaming, but is it possible for a group of American Muslims to emerge which will work selflessly in pursuit of the most important public good – the normative integrity of our public and private institutions.

Chapter 5
American Muslim Perspective

What Is the American Muslim Perspective?

And there may spring from you a nation who
invite to goodness, and enjoin right conduct
and forbid indecency. – Qur'an 3: 104 [Pickthall]

Increasingly, Muslims in America are talking about the "American Muslim Perspective" (AMP). The term is gaining currency and has even developed its own political implications, but surprisingly very little context is associated with the term. Every time I say it in meetings or seminars, there are some who look at me suspiciously. And then there are others who distinctly nod their heads in agreement. Amazing indeed. While no one has articulated what the American Muslim perspective is, it has already developed its supporters and its critics.

It is easy to identify what the critics of AMP think of it. They think that Islam is developing a new character through a dialectic interaction with American liberalism.

In the words of a young man from Chicago, "American Islam is the weak and smiley face of Islam advanced by scholars like John Esposito and Yvonne Haddad and practiced by organizations like ISNA." This bright young man, an American convert to Islam who has a law degree, helpfully elaborates further. "American Islam is controlled by Americans who are using some Muslims to redefine Islamic principles to 'fit into' American society."

Needless to say, the rethinking of Muslim relations with America, prompted by the profound realization that Islam and Muslims are here to stay, is sitting uneasily with those who live in Los Angeles but pretend they are in Lahore, or with those who live in Pittsburgh but make believe they are in Palestine. Their deep suspicions of the West extend to fellow Muslims and ideas like the AMP, which they see as "getting cozy with the Kuffar (infidels)!"

Before we even begin to talk about an AMP we need to inquire whether there is such an entity as an "American Muslim" with a distinct perspective. Hyphenated Americans are as commonplace as burgers and Coke. When one talks about African Americans, or Cuban Americans or even Asian Americans, nationality is central and ethnicity is the difference.

But in the case of American Muslims, as with American Jews, the religious identity takes precedence over the national identity and the term American Muslim signifies a special kind of a Muslim, while a Cuban American is a special type of American. Having said that, we must remember that this identity, American Muslim, is still a hypothesis until we can demonstrate that it brings some "difference" to Muslim identity.

At a vulgar level we can argue that if Muslims can be proud of associating with their "nation-states," Turkey, Iran, Pakistan, Bangladesh, then why can't American Muslims also be proud of Uncle Sam? Our lawyer friend may be tempted to respond, in a shocked tone, that Uncle Sam habitually bombs and kills Muslims all over the place. Also that many Americans and their institutions demonize Islam and suppress Islamic initiatives. So how can we identify with this out-of-control, arrogant and immoral power?

To him I can only point out the tragedies of the Muslim world. In Turkey it is forbidden for a civil servant or student or teacher to wear the hijab in a public building. But not in the U.S. Iraqi and Turkish armies have killed thousands of Muslims (Kurds) in the past few decades. The Pakistani army has killed hundreds of thousands of Muslims in Bangladesh. Afghan Muslims have killed many thousands of their fellow Muslims. The Iran-Iraq war killed many times more Muslims in a decade than America has in its entire history! The Algerian civil war has killed more Muslims in the 1990s alone. Egyptian and Syrian forces have killed more Islamic activists than America. The list could go on, but I think the point is made and I do not wish to further embarrass my fellow Muslims.

Nor should we forget that within U.S. borders there are some six million Muslims who have no plans to live anywhere else. Or if they choose otherwise they are as free to go as to stay. So if, in spite of all the carnage and massacres, it is OK to be proud Afghan, Egyptian, Syrian, Pakistani, Iranian, Iraqi, and Turkish Muslims, then there is nothing wrong in being proud American Muslims. And this pride may well be an important ingredient of the American Muslim perspective. But as I said earlier, that would be at a vulgar level. Nationalism is nothing but a modernized version of tribalism, which has remained the bane of Islam for centuries.

At a more profound level, the differences between an American Muslim and a Pakistani or Egyptian Muslim are in the "perspectives" they hold, not in their nationality. Since American Muslims enjoy high levels of educational achievement and financial stability they can and should act at least as wisely as their counterparts in the Third World.

Moreover, the relative freedom available to think and work for Islam in America can enable American Muslims to become a global force. The presence of so many Muslim intellectuals and scholars in the West is another advantage that American Muslims enjoy. Indeed the opportunity for so many Muslim ethnicities to come together, undivided by silly nationalist agendas, has after a long time reproduced in microcosm a truly global *Ummah*.

Now if this truly global *Ummah* can articulate a vision of Islam free from cultural artifacts, then we can begin to see a true turn toward an Islamic identity. The interests of this community, free from parochial particularism, can identify the foundations upon which it will be realistic to even think about a global Muslim unity.

Assuming that such an American Muslim identity is emerging, the standpoint of this community will be the American Muslim perspective. So perhaps now we can begin to get some idea about AMP. It is a global vision of Islam leading to global politics, both of which are free from the localizing influences of nationalism and ethnicity.

The American Muslim perspective is a powerful idea. If realized it has the potential to be truly transformative. It may well be the answer to the challenges that Muslims face both here and in the Muslim World. As the world becomes increasingly angry and hostile to what is now widely described as "Islamic militancy", the American Muslim perspective can become an alternate medium through which Muslims can express their desire to live as peace loving people committed deeply to the ideals of Islam. In simple terms, the American Muslim perspective is the voice of moderate Islam that many Muslims and the rest of the world are yearning for.

The Power of Ideas

"Knowledge is like sealed treasure houses, the keys for which are inquiry. Inquire therefore, for in it lies reward for four: the inquirer, the learned, the auditor and their admirer."
– Prophet Muhammad (pbuh)[3]

Human existence has always been dependent on the power of ideas. It was our capacity for ideas that allowed us to take over this planet from other beasts far more powerful than us. It is safe to say that in the very beginning of human life, the fact that ideas are more powerful than power itself was established. The impact of ideas can be felt in three different ways; firstly, ideas can transform our understanding of life and through that transform the very conditions of our existence. Secondly, ideas can transform our conception of ourselves and begin a new reconstruction of the self (*Tazkiyyah Annafs*). Finally, ideas can alter the balance of power between communities and lead to freedom from slavery and oppression (*Islah*).

Before we go any further with this discussion, let me make it clear that there are basically two types of ideas – pure ideas and contingent ideas. Pure ideas are solely the province of the supreme divine being – Allah – and in that sense the unfolding of creation is a continuous flow of ideas from the divine fountainhead. Human beings are only capable of producing contingent ideas. Contingent ideas are nothing but the outcome of the human processing of pure ideas. Pure ideas confront us in the form of revealed texts, material creation itself and as insights garnered through connections with the divine.

---

3. Reported by Imam Al Gazzali, *Ihya Ulu al-din*. See Nabih Amin Faris, *The Book of Knowledge* (New Delhi: Idara Isha'at-e-Diniyat, 1996), p. 11.

But we must remember that all contingent ideas have an expiry date. Once ideas become stale they lose their emancipatory capacity and become oppressive. Ideas that once liberated and transformed a society, if allowed to become dogma, will cause stagnation and decline of that society. Yes, you read me correctly. The same idea can liberate and imprison the individual/collective mind as well. The key to utilizing the power of ideas is to ensure that the human will is always in charge and never subordinated to any old idea.

Ideas are meanings. Without ideas nothing is meaningful. All individuals and civilizations have an idea of the self and an idea of the big picture. These constitutive ideas are essential not only for the existence but the continued growth of the self. If we allow foundational ideas to stagnate then we will lose our vitality and our strength and look like yesterdays pasta.

This is what, I believe, has happened to the Islamic *Ummah*. Our genesis, our phenomenal and explosive growth and all our past glory, was the sole expression of a divine idea – Islam. The idea of Islam transformed our vision of ourselves, gave us a new meaning of life itself, and as it unfolded we gave birth to one of the most glorious periods in human history.

The glory of the Islamic civilization emerged as a consequence of the enormous flow of contingent ideas from Muslim thinkers processing the pure idea of Islam. It led to the emergence of several streams of ideas (discourses) *fiqh* (Islamic legal thought), *falsafa* (philosophy), *adab* (moral science), *tasawwuf* (spirituality), and *kalam* (metaphysics). Islamic science that included mathematics, physics, geology, chemistry, astronomy, anthropology, sociology and historiography developed as the handmaiden of Islamic philosophy.

These streams of contingent ideas continued to flow and enrich not only the Islamic World but also the entire human civilization. Every new stream of ideas added a newer, deeper and richer dimension to the Islamic world. In its time it manifested the zenith of human achievements in both corporeal as well as spiritual sense. This great epoch in human history was essentially the outcome of the human mind processing the pure idea of Islam.

Today, the Islamic *Ummah* is in disarray. It has not only lost its past glory, but has also lost the capacity to comprehend the virtues and the causes of its past glory. It is in decline and unable to defend or take care of itself. After nearly 100 years of Islamic revivalism in the Sunni world, the best we have to show is the Taliban in Afghanistan! Let us hope that like Iran, Afghanistan too will turn towards moderation and freedom.

I believe the singular reason for this state of affairs is the transformation of a people from processors of ideas to recyclers of ideas. On the moral and spiritual front we are trying to recycle the ideas of our forefathers and on the material front we are just consumers of Western ideas.

Muslims, thanks to their obsessions with contingent ideas like the *fiqh* literature, have become estranged from the pure idea of Islam, and have also been deprived of their capacity to generate contingent ideas more meaningful to their times. It is this alienation from the creative process of idea generation that has stripped the Islamic civilization of its vitality and its brilliance leaving behind an embittered, insecure and clueless *Ummah*.

The sooner we realize the absence of ideas and encourage, freedom of thought, creativity, and intellectual self-determination, the sooner will we recover some semblance of our past glory and fulfill our God given mandate of universal moral leadership.

Changing the Parameters of Muslim Discourse

Verily never will God change the condition of a people until they change it themselves. – Qur'an 13: 11

For nearly five hundred years the Islamic civilization has existed without the global preeminence it had got used to and taken for granted. In the opinion of Muslim scholars, moral leadership is the divine mandate of Muslims, individually as well as collectively. This understanding of Islam's social purpose is easily derived from The *Qur'an*'s description of human beings as Allah's vicegerents on Earth (*Qur'an* 2: 30) who are required to encourage the good and prohibit evil (*Qur'an* 9: 112). Thus the understanding of our earthly purpose as moral leadership and the harsh contrast of Islam's secondary position in global norms, institutions and practices has, needless to say, been a source of considerable agony to Muslim intellectuals and scholars. Our inability to determine the norms that govern society does not sit well with our conception of our selves as the bearers of the "Truth" and guardians of "the "Good".

This incongruence between objectives and capabilities is resulting in several debilitating social conditions. Muslims are beginning to lower their targets. First they are giving up global objectives and settling for local ones. Instead of transforming the entire world, we have settled for the *islah* (reformation) of the *Ummah*, or the *mulk/millat* (country) or just the *muhalla* (neighborhood). Of course this is justified by arguing that this is a necessary first step. But after 1500 years, we shouldn't still be at the first step. Perhaps there is some wisdom in this approach of thinking globally but acting locally. If each individual took care of his/her local responsibility, there may be no global problems. But there must be a conscious recognition in the minds of all Muslim activists that their mission is global but their strategic imperatives are local. This will encourage a spirit of cooperation and coordination among Muslim individuals and groups. Often we get so focused on local issues that the ultimate objectives of the mission are lost.

Secondly, those frustrated and dejected with the unwavering gap between capabilities and objectives are either giving up objectives by losing faith in them, or they are resorting to means which are not permissible. In the first case Muslims are increasingly questioning the virtue of religion and are turning to secular and Western ideologies such as nationalism and liberalism, in pursuit of material comforts and individual dignity. The turn towards Kemalism in Turkey, socialism in the Arab World, and even Marxism in some intellectual sections of Muslim society, are all manifestations of a search for ideas, meanings and purpose, through intellectual emulation of the powerful and successful West – clearly a rejection of Islam. Alternatively, Muslims are resorting to force and often un-Islamic means to establish Islamic principles in society. The use of violence in Afghanistan, Algeria and other places in order to enforce adherence to Islamic principles makes a mockery of Islam and its moral claims. Moral leadership is exercised by example and by becoming worthy of emulation and not by compulsion and domination.

The third consequence of the gap between Islamic expectations and Muslim capabilities is the emergence of fragmentation. Fragmentation is occurring within the *Ummah* on the slightest pretext. The incitement for fragmentation can come from something as profound as the interpretation of texts or the character of modern Islamic polities to something as base as ethnicity or even as mundane as the length of your trousers. This fragmentation and the growing intolerance within Muslims is the most egregious consequence of weakness. Muslim leaders must recognize the short term as well as long-term implications of fragmentation and resist it by inculcating a spirit of compassion, tolerance and compromise in Muslims, at least for other Muslims. The demands of moral leadership imply that Muslims show compassion and tolerance to all, particularly the non-Muslims. But in an environment where Islam is constantly being demonized and Muslim beliefs attacked by non-Muslim media it may be difficult to expect simple Muslims to transcend their feeling of fear of the aggressor and exercise tolerance towards all. But is it too much to expect Muslims to be tolerant, compassionate and may be even affectionate towards other Muslims?

I have no simple answers to the problems of the *Ummah*. Indeed on this issue I do not have any complex suggestions either. I can make superfluous comments such as "we must unite to pool our resources and enhance our capabilities so that we can realize our goals". But that will not help. Such grandiose statements do not even win votes anymore anywhere. I however do believe that we can gradually work towards a more unified, more purposeful, more tolerant and more successful *Ummah* if the leaders of our communities, our *khatibs*, attempt to change the parameters of Muslim discourse. We stop complaining, stop attacking each other, and emphasize cooperation over conflict, stress the virtues of moderation, condemn extremism and instill a sense of self-confidence.

It is important to recognize that the parameters we impose on discourses actually begin to exercise limits on public interaction and thought. Most people interact with their social reality through discussions and arguments in informal settings. The information and perspectives on issues discussed at these informal settings are not gleaned from perusal of scholarly literature. They are often overheard. Muslims do not have formal media such as TV and newspapers where Muslim dilemmas are discussed systematically from the perspective of Muslims and in the interest of Islam. There are alternate journals but still the sources that shape Muslim sensibilities on issues from an Islamic perspective are limited to the pulpit (*minbar*). Thus if we can alter the very structures of the discourse that is launched from the minbar we can impact the nature of conversation in the private as well as public spheres of Muslim life and ultimately determine the parameters of contemporary Muslim consciousness.

So far the discourses that emerge from the minbar lack an essential quality – the correspondence between Muslim realities and a critical consensual discussion of the global Muslim condition. We are too eager to blame others for our condition. Remember that *Qur'an* tells us that Allah will not change the condition of a people unless they change it themselves (*Qur'an* 13: 11). The pulpit has become a stage from which self-righteous normative elite lectures the masses and exhorts them to do this or that. What needs to be done is to develop a more interactive relationship between the pulpit and the member of the congregation. We must invite Muslims to participate in a dialogue (not during the *Qutbah* of course) that will recruit their energies and their will in the pursuit of collective emancipation.

A deliberative process can be initiated that will employ the energies and the consent of the masses in the process of change and will also empower the minbar as well as the member. But in order to enhance the power of the pulpit and make it a transformative agent of society, we need to first achieve a general consensus amongst Muslim speakers so that they agree upon the strategy and substance of discourse. There has been a lot of talk about coordination of

Qutbahs but nothing concrete has been done. Perhaps such a dialogue between *Khateebs* in America can be initiated at conventions like ISNA's annual affair. As a community we have a powerful instrument for grass roots mobilization and diffusion of ideas. But this instrument can only serve the interests of Islam, once it has ceased to serve other interests.

Contemporary Use of Islamic Law

On no soul doth God Place a burden greater than it can bear. – Qur'an 2: 286

The American Muslim community is in its formative stages and is facing many contentious issues, such as whether to participate in American politics or not, how to deal with non-Muslims, what kind of citizen a Muslim should be in a secular democracy and how to redefine gender roles in postmodern times. Needless to say, there are many different perspectives competing to gain legitimacy and leadership to guide the emerging direction of the new community.

This process is further compounded by the resonance of Islamic resurgence in the Muslim Diaspora. Many Islamic movements are experiencing strong revival in the traditional homelands of Islam and are also influencing Islamic life in the U.S.. Some of the different movements include Islamic political movements seeking to establish the Islamic state, puritanical movements seeking to purify the faith, Sufi movements seeking to revive their *tariqas* (ways) and sectarian movements renewing old and forgotten disputes.

The enormous energy released from these movements is galvanizing Muslims everywhere leading to intense, heated discussions and debates as to how Islam and the global Islamic revival should be understood and implemented in their local context. In all these contentious discussions, more and more people are turning to the tradition of Islamic law to settle disputes and give decisive verdicts on what is right and what is wrong. Usually this is more in the form of who is right and who is wrong.

It is in this discursive environment that we must re-evaluate the relationship between Islam and Islamic law. It should be understood that the two are not identical; Islamic law is a subset of Islam. In other words, there is more to Islam than just legal injunctions.

Islam is the "shar", the way or the path revealed by God that will lead to success in this life and in the hereafter. Islam is about enlightenment above anything else. It makes a human a civilized being. Islam brings knowledge to the ignorant and discipline and direction to his/her life. Most importantly, Islam brings answers to the mysteries of being. As humans we all seek answers to perennial existential questions such as who am I? Where do I come from and what is my purpose?

Islam provides rational, substantive, empowering, enlightening and inspirational answers to these questions and many more. Islamic law is just one of the many elements of Islam. The purpose of Islamic law is not to present a set of arbitrary hurdles to test the belief of Muslims. It is a set of norms that direct an individual towards a materially and spiritually good life. It also provides constitutional principles that will help ensure justice and welfare for all as society develops political and legal institutions to manage the ever-increasing complexity of life and human interactions.

Islamic Law or the *Shariah* is not a clearly articulated set of rules available for immediate reference. This is the point where Muslims with a superficial understanding of Islamic law, or a rigid attitude towards Islamic traditions err, often with dangerous consequences. Islamic law and the extant traditions are essentially an interpretation of revealed sources, The *Qur'an* and many of the Prophet's (pbuh) guiding traditions.

There are many interpretations of the *Shariah* based upon five different schools: the Hanafi, the Shafii, the Maliki, the Hanbali and the Jaffari, which are all equally valid and legitimate. Islamic legal tradition practices epistemological pluralism that allows it to maintain that these schools may differ in their legal opinions but remain equally valid.

This enlightened quality of Islamic legal tradition is unfortunately missing from the contemporary Muslim discourse and it has been replaced by an intransigent, rigid and bellicose attitude that diminishes the virtues of the legal tradition.

The contemporary Islamic revival is taking place when the human history itself is in tremendous flux. We are experiencing the simultaneous play of traditional, modern and postmodern forces. In this atmosphere, when Muslims debate the essence of Islamic identity, the present attitude toward assuming that any interpretation of Islamic law is absolute and non-negotiable, acts as a barrier rather than as a facilitator of inter Muslim dialogue.

If Muslims wish to unite and revive the great spirit of Islam and its civilizing ethos, then we must learn to be more tolerant and more open minded in our approach to contending arguments. Strength, legitimacy and vitality come from openness, tolerance of difference and from the willingness to create rather than burn bridges.

As more and more Muslims turn towards Islam in search of meaning and direction, there will be a powerful need to reexamine Islamic tradition and the Islamic message in the light of our present existential conditions. Muslims now come from different cultures and different political and economic conditions. Their interpretations of what it means to live according to Islam will differ. While there will be a need for consensus on some issues like political governance, there can be room for difference in other areas.

For all this to work it is important that Muslims develop an ethics of discourse. The present rigid and inflexible approach to Islamic legal opinions of the past must be discarded and replaced with a more open and compassionate understanding of Islam.

Islamic law is supposed to serve the Muslim society. It cannot do so by imposing itself on the society. Remember God is not a tyrant; He is most merciful and most benevolent. It is those who are supercilious enough to speak on his behalf that often suffer from this affliction.

Muslim Women; What Can Be Done?

And for women are rights over men similar to those of men over women. – Qur'an 2: 228

The changes and challenges of the twentieth century have indeed been rough for Muslim women. They have been caught in the crossfire at many levels. Whether it is the culture wars between Islam and the West, or the civil wars between secularists and Islamists, Muslim women have to bear the brunt of travails associated with these conflicts. Either they lose their husbands and sons on the battlefield, or they lose their freedoms and dignity in the social arena. Tragedy and irony are the two dominant themes of their existence. At times, they are victims of those who seek to protect them and at other times, those who seek to emancipate them, oppress them. Even when it comes to historical processes, Muslim women are caught in the struggle between the imperialism of modernity and the intransigence of traditions.

In Afghanistan, the Talibanization of Islam had many consequences. Some good, like restoring a modicum of stability to a region devastated by war, and some bad, particularly the assault on the civil liberties of women. In the name of Islam, a religion that began when God asked Prophet Muhammad to, "Iqra" (read), the Taliban had systematically sought to deprive women of education, the essence of emancipation. In Turkey, to protect civil society from the so-called evils of religion, secular-democrats are using batons to keep Muslim women who where the *hijab* (headscarf) out of schools, and universities. In France, the land where the modern project of freedom began with a glorious revolution, and where the new standards of fashion are set, politicians are keeping Muslim women with hijab out of schools for sartorial reasons. East or West, secular or religious, all forces seem determined to preclude the emancipation of Muslim women.

We live in a highly interdependent world. What happens in the economic or the political arena has critical impact on the social stage. Changes in the East and moods in the West influence each other profoundly. As Muslims struggle to recover from the effects of colonialism, their societies cry out for political and social change. Since change in the East endangers Western hegemony, any attempts at change become a political threat. The West opposes political initiatives in the East, whether Islamism or Socialism. Social initiatives from the West, feminism or liberalism, threaten the politics of the East and are in turn rejected. The site for these battles, cultural and political, invariably ends up on the Muslim woman's head, literally!

So far, most of the rescue attempts have come from the West. But the humanitarian concern for the plight of Muslim Women is often accompanied by an attendant discourse that demonizes Islam. It confuses issues and makes most Muslims suspicious. They imagine these projects as another attempt to degrade Islam and ridicule Muslim beliefs. Western double standards also hurt the prospects for change. Muslims who are willing to work with Western agencies to improve the conditions of Muslim women are forced to retreat in the face of these double standards. For example, when the Taliban use ideological rhetoric to deprive Muslim women access to basic education, Western media and agencies condemn them justifiably, and also attack Islam, unnecessarily. But when the French and Turks do the same by using ideology to deprive Muslim women access to education, there is little done to remedy the situation. Recently, the "secular state" of Turkey actually took away the citizenship of one of its nationally elected representatives because she dared to cover her head, and most of the Western world, otherwise quick to rush to the aid of Muslim women, did not do much to prevent it.

Unfortunately, Muslim feminists do not help their cause either. Muslim feminists are broadly of two types, extremely westernized or too traditional. The Westernized Muslim feminists generate a discourse that mimics their Western counterparts. Their extreme Westernization, in worldview as well as life-style, not only scares the traditional Muslim male but also most Muslim women. As a result, the projects and goals they advocate are delegitimized purely because of their manifest disregard and disrespect for Islam and traditional Muslim values. Of course they do win many supporters and admirers among Western feminists and the liberal establishment, but this does little to ameliorate the plight of Muslim women.

The so-called Islamic feminists occupy the other extreme pole. They seem to be reacting to the absence of "Islam" in Westernized feminists, whom they perceive as a threat to Islamic heritage and the institutions of family, marriage and modesty. They expire their resources and energies in defending traditional practices and martyr the project of women's emancipation in the defense of an Islam, articulated by Muslim orthodoxy. Thus, while the Western Muslim feminists are busy learning the "lingo" and admiring their Western counterparts, the Islamic feminists are busy confirming the stereotypes. The regular Muslim woman meanwhile continues to suffer. Muslim men at the moment are engrossed in preparing for civilizational clashes or civilizational dialogues. They cannot pay any attention to the condition of Muslim women, while the Muslim man is still enslaved and Muslim lands are still under attack.

Is there anything that we can do? Yes. American Muslims can launch several initiatives. First and foremost, we must launch an educational campaign among American Muslims that women in some parts of the Muslim world do not have access to their Islamic rights. It does not mean that we are saying Islam is inferior to the West. We should not be reactionary to anybody's critique of the condition of Muslim women. Second, we must try to increase awareness among Muslims everywhere about women's rights to education, equality, dignity, and freedom of choice and action. The language of rights may engender negative reactions and therefore, appropriate Qur'anic and *Hadith* literature should be made available. American Muslims must provide the intellectual and financial resources necessary for this global project since no one else may contribute.

Finally, American Muslims must help initiate an awakening among Muslims to the overwhelming domination of men in Islamic legal studies. There is no doubt in my mind that when men alone interpret the *Qur'an* and *Hadith* and Islamic juristic traditions, they do it from a masculine perspective. It is important that we produce more and more women scholars of Islam who can eventually understand and advance their own understanding of Islamic sources.

If there can be so many differences between the understanding of men that we have at least five different legal traditions (*madhahib*) and so many methodologies (*tarikas*) from *Salafi* to Sufi, from *Wahabi* to *Barelvi*, from *Tablighi Jamaat* to *Jamaate-Islami*, then surely women too will have a different understanding of Muslim sources.

Islamic thinkers (men) themselves have acknowledged that men and women have fundamentally different natures. While men tend to be absolutist, women tend towards infinity. When men emphasize justice, women encourage mercy and tolerance. When men pursue knowledge, women seek understanding. Remember both these characteristics, masculine and feminine are human manifestations of divine attributes. And just as justice without mercy can be cruel, masculine understanding without feminine input can also become harsh. It is time we encouraged more women scholars of Islam and explicitly seek their understanding of Islam. This will only strengthen the *Ummah* and enrich us.

Women and Islamic Law

They are a garment to you and you are a garment to them. – Qur'an 2:187

Some Muslim countries like Turkey (Tancu Ciller), Pakistan (Benazir Bhutto) and Bangladesh (Khalida Zia) have had women heads of state. But this remarkable fact does not do justice to the extent to which Muslim women are marginalized from the Muslim public sphere. A quick survey of Islamic associations like Islamic Society of North America (ISNA), Islamic Circle of North America (ICNA), Islamic organizations like the American Muslim Council (AMC), Council on American and Islamic Relations (CAIR), and one will find that women have never headed these organizations. The Association of Muslim Social Scientists (AMSS), a clearly more enlightened of Muslim institutions in America, too has never had a woman President in thirty years of its existence. This is not unique to North America; Women continue to remain absent from leadership and responsible positions in Islamic societies everywhere.

Even though there is evidence in the *Qur'an* (2: 228) that would allow men and women to be treated equally, Islamic legal tradition has over the centuries circumscribed the role of women in the public sphere. Islamic legal scholars have constantly evoked Qur'anic injunctions for modesty and limited the public role of Muslim women. The *Qur'an* also makes similar demands of modesty from men and women (*Qur'an* 24: 31), but the modesty issue has been instrumental in diminishing the public role of women but not men. If the demands of modesty limit women's access to the public arena then the same demands should also limit the role of men. But Islamic scholars, who are usually male, have limited the scope of Qur'anic verses itself based on a culturally influenced understanding of the Qur'anic concept of modesty.

All the injunctions of The *Qur'an*, to struggle in the name of Islam, to establish justice (*Qur'an* 55: 9), and to eliminate tyranny, are addressed to both men and women. These Islamic injunctions stem from the Qur'anic revelation that God has appointed both men and women as his vicegerents on Earth (*Qur'an* 2: 30). When God commanded in the *Qur'an* to do good and forbid evil (*Qur'an* 9: 112), he did not prescribe different functions for men and women. How can women then fulfill their Islamic mandate if their public role is restricted?

Interestingly most Muslim intellectuals and scholars insist that Islam is a holistic religion. We reject secularism on the grounds that in Islam religion and politics are not separate, and neither are public and private spheres since both are within the juristic purview of Islamic injunctions. But if we were to exclude women from public life, then their religious manifestations would remain essentially private and Islam for them will remain a private affair.

How can this condition be remedied and an attempt to emancipate the Muslim woman be initiated so that she can live her life as a complete *Muslima*, struggling for good and justice in the private as well as the public arena? This then is our problematic.

Western feminist perspectives have an easy answer. Reject Islam, a patriarchic system, and live life worshipping the self. Their solutions essentially liberate woman by incarcerating God within the boundaries of feminine desire to replicate masculine achievements. Most sensible and practicing Muslims, men and women, reject this philosophy that glosses over the differences between men and women as socially constructed and reconstructs the woman in the image of the man, with identical desires and ambitions and measures of success.

What we need is an authentic Islamic critique of the present understanding of women's role in an Islamic society and to advance an emancipatory discourse from within the Islamic tradition. I am calling for an *Ijtihad* that critically evaluates how Islamic tradition has reached the conclusions that it maintains about the limited public role of women.

Ijtihad is an Islamic legal instrument that allows an Islamic scholar to exercise personal reasoning in understanding the Divine Law (*Shariah*) whenever it is not explicit. Islamic legal scholars go down a hierarchy of sources before they give a ruling on any issue. They look in to the *Qur'an*, and then the Prophetic traditions, then the consensus (*Ijma*) of the companions of the Prophet and the early scholars. When an answer cannot be found in all these sources only then the scholar uses his reasoning to deduce Islamic ruling on a particular issue while remaining within the confines of Islamic sensibilities.

It is still possible for two scholars who use the same method to reach different conclusions on the same issues. For example scholars of the Maliki school of Law discourage Muslims from living in non-Muslim societies and ask them to migrate from there to Muslim lands; Whereas, scholars of the Hanafi school, encourage migration to non-Muslim lands, for missionary purposes. Islamic law recognizes this possibility and accepts an epistemological pluralism that has led to the establishment of different but equally valid schools of law. There are five differing but valid interpretations of Islamic principles. Male thinkers and jurists advanced all these schools of thought. None of the formative legal scholars has been a woman.

There is nothing in the Islamic sources that explicitly prohibits Muslim women from exercising their right to understand Islam independently and advance independent opinions and claim equal validity with the existing schools. The domination of men in legal studies has historically prevented this from happening.

Today, women are more aware of their marginal status. They also know that in the time of the Prophet (pbuh) and the rightly guided Caliphs, women played a significant role in the public sphere. The Prophet's wife Aysha (rah) was prominent in the public sphere of her time. She was frequently consulted on major issues and she even went to war.

But today, except in Turkey and in South Asia, were Muslim Women have been Prime Ministers, women remain insignificant in the Arab World in particular and the rest of the Muslim World in general.

The only way the Muslim women's condition can be improved from within the Islamic tradition is if we have more women scholars of Islam, interpreting Islamic law and history with the explicit interest of emancipating women. This is easily said then done. Muslim legal scholars will resist this intrusion on their sovereignty vehemently and will call all such attempts as unIslamic and motivated by the West to destroy Islam and Islamic family structure.

In this brief discussion, I will suggest the first step that women intellectuals and scholars can take. Then the ball is in their court.

There are two types of *ijtihad*: *ijtihad* of law and *Ijtihad* of fact. The former process extracts Islamic rulings from Islamic sources and the second investigates factual circumstances. For example consider a ruling such as "X cannot be an Imam since X is a disbeliever". This simple ruling includes two kinds of legal investigation. The first, that according to Islamic law one has to be a believer to be able to lead prayers and the second, a factual investigation that X is indeed a disbeliever. While legal scholars may have more authority than others when it comes to *ijtihad* of law, *ijtihad* of fact is the domain of one who is in possession of true facts.

Therefore I contend that when it comes to articulating specific Islamic rulings about women's role, male Islamic legal scholars may be able to articulate laws in general, but they cannot become specific because they are not in possession of facts about the "feminine experience". Only women therefore should be qualified to do *ijtihad* of facts concerning women's issues.

This is the first step, banish male opinion and judgments about women's experiences. Muslim women must represent themselves in matters of determining women's experiences for the purpose of extracting Islamic rulings.

The second step would be for women to acquire education and Islamic legal expertise and gradually take over the function of doing *ijtihad* of law that concerns women as well as anything else that they may wish to comment on.

One is beginning to see the trend already. Dr. Azizah Al-Hibri is an Islamic legal scholar at Richmond University, who researches women's as well as political issues. Dr. Amira Sonbol at Georgetown University teaches the history of Arab law. Amina Mohsin Wudud writes on Women's issues and teaches at the Virginia Common Wealth University. A recent book edited by Gisela Webb and published by Syracuse University Press, *Windows of Faith*, gives a voice to several Muslim women activist – scholars in North America. There are many younger Muslim women studying law and getting ready to participate in Islamic legal tradition, particularly in the U.S.. American Muslims must encourage and support them and who knows one day we may even have an Islamic feminist legal school.

Chapter 6

Reflections on
Islam and Democracy

Islam and Democracy

*Oh you who believe, Obey Allah and obey
the apostle and those who are entrusted with
authority from among you.* – Qur'an 4: 59

Two extremely different groups, one from the West and one
from the Muslim World, have been arguing vehemently that
Islam and Democracy are incompatible.

On one hand some western scholars and ideologues have tried to
present Islam as an anti-democratic and inherently authoritarian ethos
that precludes democratization in the Muslims World. By misrepre-
senting Islam in this way they are seeking to prove that Islam as a set
of values is inferior to Western liberalism and is indeed a barrier to the
global progress of civilization. This argument is also helpful to Israel,
which regardless of its egregious human rights violations against
Palestinians, continues to enjoy the reputation as the sole democracy
in the Middle East. Positioned as a solitary defender of democracy in
the Middle East, Israel enjoys immense moral and military support of
the West, which includes overlooking its dismal human rights record
against Arabs. As an "in principle advocate of democracy" Israel with
its horrible record is preferred over Islam that has an exemplary
history of tolerance and freedom but is presented as "in principle
antithetical to democracy".

On the other hand many Islamic activists, using extremely broad,
simple and sometimes crude notions of secularism and sovereignty,
reject democracy as rule of Man as opposed to Islam that is rule
of God. But for the purpose of reflection let me merely suggest that
Islamists who reject democracy falsely assume that secularism and

democracy are necessarily connected. Secularism is a liberal tradition not a prerequisite for democracy. Religion does play a significant role in democratic politics. The contemporary U.S. is a case in point. These Islamists also do not make a distinction between dejure sovereignty and defacto sovereignty. For example even though God was supposedly sovereign in Afghanistan, in fact it is the Taliban who were sovereign there.

In order to understand the situation better one has to recognize the difference between sovereignty in principle and sovereignty in fact. Sovereignty in fact is always Man's whether in a democracy or an Islamic State. Rejecting democracy because Man is sovereign is a big mistake. What we really need to worry about is how to limit the defacto sovereignty of Man. Democracy with its principles of limited government, public accountability, checks and balances, separation of powers and transparency in governance does succeed in limiting Man's sovereignty. The Muslim world plagued by despots, dictators and self-regarding monarchs badly needs the limitation of man's sovereignty.

Here I shall explore only one contention; the idea that democracy is absent in the Muslim World because of Islam. Secular fundamentalists who believe that Islam and democracy are incompatible argue that in order to democratize the Muslim world needs to either discard the project of Islamization and liberalize or essentially reform Islam itself to accommodate democracy. This argument is based on one theoretical assumption that democracy and *shura* (Islam) are not compatible and one empirical assumption that Muslims strongly adhere to Islamic principles.

For the purpose of argument let us concede the theoretical assumption that Islam and democracy are incompatible. But in order to argue that democracy is missing from the Islamic world because of Islam, it must be demonstrated that Muslims indeed practice Islam. One of the primary motivations for the contemporary Islamic revival is the widespread belief, even consensus, among Muslims that their societies have strayed far away from Islam. A brief survey of adherence to the personal and public obligatory aspects of Islam such as establishment of prayer, fasting and charity, and establishment of justice, crime and corruption free virtuous societies; will reveal that Muslim societies are not only undemocratic but also unIslamic. So why blame Islam if unIslamic societies are also undemocratic?

Let me also point out that there are more nations in the Muslim world that claim to be democratic – Bangladesh, Kuwait, Jordan, Turkey, Iran, Pakistan, Malaysia, Egypt, Indonesia, Tunisia, Algeria, Nigeria – than Islamic – Iran, Saudi Arabia, Pakistan, Afghanistan, Malaysia and Sudan. Half of the self proclaimed Islamic states also claim to be democracies. The point is simple; contrary to the claims otherwise, the democratic ideal is quite widely upheld in the Muslim world.

Even prominent Islamic revivalists of the twentieth century like Maulana Maududi and Imam Khomeni have advocated the cause of democracy. Maulana Maududi was the first to write about the concept of a theodemocracy – a God centered democratic polity. And Imam Khomeini established separation of powers, parliament, elections and public accountability along with the institution of *Vilayat-e-faqi* after the Islamic revolution of Iran.

I believe that there is nothing in Islam and in Muslim practices that is fundamentally opposed to democracy – justice, freedom, fairness, equality or tolerance. There are a few Muslims who reject democracy. But they do so only because they falsely allow the modern West the ownership of a universal value. They reject democracy only because they reject the West. The large number of Muslims who came out to vote in the Presidential elections in the U.S. and those Muslims who vote in hundreds of millions in Pakistan, Bangladesh, Iran, Malaysia, Indonesia, Turkey, Egypt and elsewhere testify to their comfort with democracy. In the minds of these nearly one billion Muslims who practice some form of democracy there is no dispute between Islam and democracy.

It is time we moved onto a more fruitful line of inquiry. If not Islam what has precluded the democratization of the Muslim world? There are structural failures in the Muslim societies due to the legacy of colonialism and the debilitating corruption that preceded and made the Muslim world colonizable. Can we find a way to remove these seeds of underdevelopment?

I hope that in the years to come American Muslim institutions like the Center for the Study of Islam and Democracy and the Association of Muslim Social Scientists will focus on this line of inquiry. If they can pinpoint the structural problems that prevent the political and economic development of the Muslim World they will accomplish a great task. Policy solutions sensitive to local conditions can then emerge to tackle the prevalence of underdevelopment. I invite all American Muslims to join us in this monumental endeavor. I also invite those Islamists who are opposed to democracy to rise above ideological posturing and work with us to develop a vibrant, open, prosperous and healthy Muslim World. Once we create this open, Muslim society that has room for all visions of Islam, then we can return to debating each other about whose understanding of Islam is better. Until then let's join forces to build a free Muslim society. Free from tyranny, poverty, corruption, illiteracy, injustice and also, we must not forget, from the humiliating domination of the West. We need to emancipate the Muslim world, from the self as well as the other.

The Compact of Madina and its Democratic Foundations

He who obeys the Messenger,
has indeed obeyed Allah. – Qur'an 4: 80 [Shakir]

The Qur'an was sent as a divine guidance to those who believe and contains principles and guidelines essential for social, political and spiritual guidance for all humanity. The Qur'an should however not be mistaken as a manual. It is an essence of divine values, a collection of revealed principles the understanding and following of which will lead us along the straight path.

The derivation of a manual from the divine principles is one of the most important responsibilities that come from being a Muslim. This responsibility is like a *fard-e-kifaya*. It is enough that someone take up this task in a given place and time. As Muslims are always in search of political autonomy and ethical authenticity we repeatedly return to Islamic sources in order to derive a manual for our times from the divine principles in the *Qur'an* and the *Sunnah*.

One of the projects that contemporary Muslims are dealing with is the construction of a theory of an Islamic state. Several theories of the Islamic state have already been advanced. Some are more focused on the principle of *shura* and hence are more democratic in character while other theories are more focused on the divine authority of the *Khalifa* and are therefore more authoritarian models.

In this essay I wish to point out to one particular precedent set by Prophet Muhammad (pbuh) that not only supports the democratic theories of Islamic state but also provides a very important occasion for the development of political theory itself. The occasion I am referring to is the compact of Madina, some scholars also refer to it as the *Dastur al-Madina* (The Constitution of Madina).

We must remember that everything the Prophet said and did is essentially an exegesis of the *Qur'an*. The Prophet's actions should be understood as an interpretation, a prophetic and divine interpretation of the *Holy Qur'an*.

After Prophet Muhammad (pbuh) migrated from Makkah to Yathrib in 622 CE, he established the first Islamic state. For ten years Prophet Muhammad was not only the leader of the emerging Muslim *Ummah* in Arabia but also the political head of Madina. As the leader of Madina Prophet Muhammad exercised jurisdiction over Muslims as well as non-Muslims within the city.

The legitimacy of his rule over Madina was based on his status as the Prophet of Islam as well as on the basis of the Compact of Madina. As Prophet of Allah (swt) he had sovereignty over all Muslims by divine decree so profoundly manifest in the *Shahadah* – *Lailaha Illallah Muhammadur Rasoolullah* (There is no God but Allah and Muhammad is his messenger). When Muslims declare their faith, they not only assert the sole divinity of Allah but also the sovereignty of Muhammad as his messenger and agent on Earth.

But Muhammad (saw) did not rule over the non-Muslims of

Madina because he was the messenger of Allah. They did not recognize this particular credential of his. He ruled over them by virtue of the tri-partite compact that was signed by the *Mahajirun* (Muslim immigrants from Makkah), the *Ansar* (indigenous Muslims of Madina and the *Yahud* (Jews). It is interesting to note that Jews were partners in the making of the first Islamic state.

The compact of Madina provides an excellent historical example of two theoretical constructs that have shaped contemporary political theory and should therefore be of great value to those scholars who are involved in the theorizing of the Islamic state.

Political theory relies heavily on the ideas of a social contract and a constitution. A social contract, made famous by the French philosopher Rousseau is an imaginary agreement between people in the state of nature that leads to the establishment of a community or a state. In the state of nature people are free and are not obliged to follow any rules or laws. They are essentially sovereign individuals. But through the social contract they surrender their individual sovereignty to the collective and create the community or the state. This state then acts as an agent of the sovereign people, exercising the sovereignty that has been delegated to it by the people through the social contract in order to realize the wishes of the people enshrined in the objectives of the social contract.

While Western political thinkers like Rousseau and Locke have used this idea of an imaginary social contract as a fundamental premise for theorizing the modern state, there are really very few real examples of such an event in human history. In the American history, the Mayflower Compact – signed on the boat Mayflower in 1620 by early immigrants to America, is one example. The writing and signing of the American constitution after six months of deliberation in Philadelphia, from May to September 1787, may be considered as another example of a social contract.

But Muslims are fortunate to have the compact of Madina as a tradition upon which the foundations of a modern state can be built.

The second idea that underpins political theory is the concept of the constitution. In many ways the constitution is the document that enshrines the conditions of the social contract upon which any society is founded. The writing of a constitution is a very old idea. Aristotle himself had collected over 300 written constitutions in his lifetime.

The compact of Madina clearly served a constitutional function since it was the constitutive document for the first Islamic state. Thus we can argue that the compact of Madina serves the dual function of a social contract and a constitution.

Clearly the compact of Madina by itself cannot serve as a modern constitution. It would be quite inadequate since it is a historically specific document and quite limited in its scope. However it can serve as a guiding principle to be emulated rather than a manual to be duplicated.

The compact of Madina also illustrates what should be the relationship between the revelation and a constitution. Muhammad (saw) if he so wished could have merely indicated the truth revealed by Allah (swt) shall serve as the constitution of Madina or the basis for the new community and force this revelation upon non-Muslims. But if he did that then he would have ruled Madina with the authority of Allah behind him but without the complete consent of those under his rule.

Muhammad (saw) in his great wisdom demonstrated a democratic spirit quite unlike the authoritarian tendencies of many of those who claim to imitate him today. He chose to draw up a historically specific constitution based on the eternal and transcendent principles revealed to him and sought the consent of all who would be affected by its implementation.

In simple terms, the first Islamic state established in Madina was based on a social contract, was constitutional in character and the ruler ruled with the explicit written consent of all the citizens of the state.

Today we need to emulate Muhammad and draw up our own constitutions, historically and temporally specific to our conditions and based on the eternal and transcendent principles revealed by Allah (swt). We can use the compact of Madina as an example of how to develop manuals from principles. In conclusion, I would like to summarize the principles manifest in Prophet Muhammad's (saw) constitution of Madina. I recommend that all Muslims read this wonderful document themselves.

The Constitution of Madina establishes the importance of consent and cooperation for governance. According to this compact Muslims and non-Muslims are equal citizens of the Islamic state, with identical rights and duties. Communities with different religious orientations enjoy religious autonomy. Which essentially is wider in scope than the modern idea of religious freedom. The constitution of Madina established a pluralistic state – a community of communities. It promised equal security to all and all were equal in the eyes of the law.

The principles of equality, consensual governance and pluralism are beautifully enmeshed in the compact of Madina. It is amazing to see how Muhammad's (saw) interpretation of the *Qur'an* and the *Maqasid al-Shariah* was so democratic, so tolerant and compassionate, while contemporary Muslims' interpretation of the same is so harsh, so authoritarian and so intolerant.

I hope this discussion will invite us to look at the *Sunnah* of our dear Prophet Muhammad (saw), more closely. We must learn from him not only the principles of faith but also human virtues of mercy, compassion, equality, justice and tolerance. The constitution of Madina is an excellent manifestation of the Prophet's affinity to democracy and governance by consent.

Islamic State And Religious Minorities

So let the people of the Gospel judge by that which Allah has revealed therein, for he who judges not by that which Allah has revealed is a sinner. – Qur'an 5: 47

Today there are at least three major conceptions of religious states – Jewish, Islamic and Hindu. Israel strongly identifies itself as a Jewish state; Nepal is a Hindu state and India under the growing influence of Hindu Nationalism is toying with the idea of

Ram Rajya – Hindu statehood. Iran, Pakistan, Saudi Arabia, Malaysia, Sudan and Afghanistan under Taliban claimed to be Islamic states.

Religious states face a significant challenge from diversity. They seek to advance and establish a specific normative social agenda. In order for these states to be successful it is important that the population share the ideological beliefs of those who hold power. The presence of diversity and difference of opinion between the populace makes it necessary for the state to privilege one element of the citizenry over others thereby institutionalizing discrimination and intolerance.

Islamic states inevitably treat non-Muslim citizens as less than equal curbing their access to power and religious freedom. Even in Israel, which is a democracy, religious minorities face discrimination. In 1976 when Israel captured Jerusalem, 28% of its population was Christian and now only 2% of Jerusalem's inhabitants are Christians. Christians may become extinct in their own holy city and the primary reason for this is the religious importance of Jerusalem to the Jewish state. This is a sobering example of how in spite of democracy a religious state can marginalize religious minorities.

Malaysia is an example where religious ideology and democracy mix very well. Malaysia is 65% Muslim and strongly identifies itself as an Islamic state. It is a very active member of OIC (Organization of Islamic Conferences). In spite of its Islamic identity, Malaysian Muslims share power and wealth with Christians, Buddhists and Hindus who are all equal citizens of the country and have equal rights and duties.

But religious minorities in some Islamic states suffer institutionalized discrimination because of these states' legalist orientation and their obsession with the Islamic jurisprudence. Some of the legalist positions in Islamic states are so strict that non-Muslim minorities find it a challenge to live normal lives. Blasphemy laws and apostasy laws are well known for the problems they cause minorities. Narrow interpretation of the role of women in Islamic societies has also restricted the scope of possibilities for non-Muslim women.

The *Maqasid* al *Shariah* (the objective of the Islamic law/way) is *falah* (welfare) and *hayat-e-tayyabah* (good life) for the members of the community. But when contemporary Islamists operationalize this divine vision of the Islamic state, they define the Islamic state as that which implements the Islamic law. Islamic law is divine in its origin, and since God does not need the consent of His creation, contemporary Islamists insist on imposing Islamic law even without consent. Due to colonization, and prior to it, due to the decline of Islamic intelligentsia, Islamic legal tradition remains fossilized and is still struck in the middle ages. Islamic state therefore becomes reduced to a coercive institution seeking to enforce a system of laws that were deduced from Islamic sources several centuries ago.

The irony of this reality is that in seeking to impose Islamic law and create an Islamic state, Islamists are actually in direct opposition to the spirit and letter of the *Qur'an*. The *Qur'an* is very explicit when it says "there is no compulsion in religion," (*Qur'an* 2: 256). Elsewhere the *Qur'an* exhorts Jews to live by the laws revealed to them in the Torah. In fact The *Qur'an* expresses surprise that some Jews sought the arbitration of the Prophet of Islam (peace be upon him) rather than their own legal tradition (5: 43). The *Qur'an* also orders Christians to live by their faith; "So let the people of the Gospel judge by that which Allah has revealed therein, for he who judges not by that which Allah has revealed is a sinner," (*Qur'an* 5: 47). From these verses it is abundantly clear that an Islamic state must advocate religious pluralism even to the extent of permitting multiple legal systems.

Democratic polities are much better at dealing with minorities who do not subscribe to state ideology because they are based on constitutional guarantees of human rights conceived at the level of the individual – the smallest minority. In a sense on some issues, such as the bill of rights in the American system – the individual overrules even the majority opinion. Contemporary Islamic states have yet to develop a legal framework that ensures that there is no compulsion in religion and no discrimination against religious minorities even though the above-identified sources provide a clear Qur'anic foundation for guaranteeing religious freedom beyond even the scope of the American bill of rights.

Unlike the present day Islamists, Prophet Muhammad (pbuh), when he established the first Islamic state in Madina – actually a Jewish-Muslim federation extended to religious minorities the rights that are guaranteed to them in the *Qur'an*. Prophet Muhammad's Madina was based on the covenant of Madina, a real and actual social contract agreed upon by Muslims, Jews and others that treated them as equal citizens of Madina. They enjoyed the freedom to choose the legal system they wished to live under. Jews could live under Islamic law, or Jewish law or pre-Islamic Arab tribal traditions. There was no compulsion in religion even though Madina was an Islamic state. The difference between Madina and today's Islamic states is profound. The state of Madina was based on a real social contract that applied divine law but only in consultation and with consent of all citizens regardless of their faith. But contemporary Islamic states apply Islamic law without consent or consultation and often through coercion.

It is a sad commentary on contemporary Islamists that while democracy is a challenge to contemporary Islamic states, it was constitutive to the first Islamic state in Madina established by the Prophet of Islam.

Shura and Democracy

*Who conduct their affairs by mutual Consultation;
his reward is due from God.* – Qur'an 42: 38-40

Many scholars and intellectuals who claim that Islam contains democratic principles have singled out the principle of *shura* to illustrate their point. In this discussion I would like to examine the similarities and dissimilarities between *shura* and democracy while reserving my judgment on whether Islam and democracy are compatible.

Shura is basically a decision making process – consultative decision-making – that is considered either obligatory or desirable by Islamic scholars. Those scholars who choose to emphasize the Qur'anic verse: ".and consult with them on the matter" (3: 159) consider *shura* as obligatory, but those scholars who emphasize the verse wherein "those who conduct their affairs by counsel" (42: 38) are praised, consider *shura* as desirable. Remember the first verse directly addressed a particular decision of the Prophet and spoke to him directly, but the second verse is more in the form of a general principle. Perhaps this is the reason why, traditional Islamic scholars have never considered consultation as a necessary and legitimizing element of decision making.

What is remarkable is that the search for direct verses as proofs, and its eminent absence, has prevented Islamic scholars from reaching a decisive conclusion that *shura* is obligatory. So far the scholars are still debating the issue. There are those who suggest that the Prophet (pbuh) always consulted before making his decisions. But consider the decision to sign the *Sulah Hudaybiyah*, the Prophet (pbuh) consulted his companions but chose to act independently, clearly illustrating that consultation is non-binding. Actually there are very few instances on record when the Prophet has consulted his companions and acted upon their advise against his own wisdom. The decision to step out of Madina to engage the Meccan army is one such instance.

Thus we remain in a limbo. There is no doubt that *shura* is the Islamic way of making decisions. But is it necessary and obligatory? Will an organization or a government that does not implement a consultative process become illegitimate? We do not have a decisive answer to that issue. One thing is clear though; that more and more Muslim intellectuals are agreeing that consultative and consensual governance is the best way to govern. Jurists, however, remain either conservative or ambivalent on the topic. Many of them depend on non-consultative bodies for their livelihood and even their religious prestige and they are in no hurry to deprive themselves of the privileges that non-consultative governments extend to them. Thus in a way they are implicated in the delay in the public recognition that governments in Muslim societies must consult to retain their legitimacy.

But assuming that *shura* becomes the norm for Islamic institutions, movements and governments, does that automatically imply that democratization will follow? I am hopeful but skeptical. I do not believe that *shura* and democracy are the same kinds of institutions.

It is my sense that *shura* and democracy differ in three basic ways:

(1) unlike *shura* democracy allows modification of foundational texts. You can amend the constitution but not the *Qur'an* or the *Sunnah*. While on the face of it this does not seem like a problem, since Muslims are by definition supposed to accept the primary sources of Islam. In practice one is not dealing with the sources but the medieval interpretations of these sources and *shura* is for all purposes subordinated to the past understanding of Islamic texts.

(2) *Shura* remains non-binding while democratic process and laws are binding and can only be reversed through a democratic process and not by unilateral and oligopolistic processes.

(3) The way *shura* is discussed in Islamic discourses, it seems to me that it is something that the leader/ruler initiates and is expected to do. *Shura* is the leader consulting some people; it is not clearly whom, scholars, relatives, or the entire adult *Ummah*. Will women be consulted too? How about gays and lesbians and non-Muslims. Maybe people of these "types" can be labeled as "legal and illegal aliens," as millions are in the U.S., and legitimately excluded from the *Shura*. This issue needs to be explored and clarified. Democracy on the other hand is people consulting among themselves about who will govern and how. Notice how *shura* is top-down and democracy bottom-up.

Finally I would like to say that *shura* like democracy is a deeply contested notion, it is the successful and just practice and institutionalization of these ideas that counts rather than theoretical finessing. Unfortunately we do not reflect on these issues seriously. Moreover we must include more and more Muslims in the process to make this theoretical reflection itself a *shuratic* process. We must however be careful not to use the debate between the similarities and dissimilarities of *shura* and democracy as a surrogate for concluding if democracy and Islam are compatible or not. There is more in Islam than *shura* when it comes to reflecting over the nature of good governance and best polities. But we shall reserve that discussion for another occasion.

It is possible for us to have a global conference involving all representative scholars to have an *ijma* on the nature of *shura*. The principle of *maslaha* – public interest – can be invoked to declare *shura* as binding and legitimizing standard for Islamic governance. But to organize such a conference requires vision. Perhaps American Muslims can provide such a vision in the near future.

Sovereignty in Islam as Human Agency

Behold, thy Lord said to the angels:
"I will create a vicegerent on earth." – Qur'an 2: 30

...O David! We did indeed made thee a
vicegerent on earth: so judge thou between people
in truth (and justice)...   – Qur'an 38: 26

There is a general consensus among Islamic scholars and Muslim laymen that Islam places sovereignty in God. The *Qur'an* explicitly describes God as *Al-Malik* meaning sovereign and *Al-Malik-ul-Mulk* the eternal possessor of sovereignty. These two attributes are also among the ninety-nine names of God. The *Qur'an* (51: 58) also makes it clear beyond any doubt that all power lies in God; who is *Al-Muqtadir* – possessor of all power. Various Muslim political thinkers like Maulana Maududi, Syed Qutb, Ayatollah Khomeini and Ali Shariati have argued that the basic distinction between Western polity and Islamic polity is that while the former places sovereignty in either the state or in Man through the notion of popular sovereignty, the latter places it absolutely in God. Thus a simple explanation of the Islamic polity would be that God is sovereign and he is the source of all legislation in the form of *Al-Qur'an*.

The Islamic state will base its precepts on Islamic law and constitution, the *Shariah*, which is derived from the *Qur'an* and *Hadith*. The Caliph, vicegerent will rule on behalf of God and his endeavor shall be to implement and enforce the *Shariah*. The *Qur'an* repeatedly emphasizes the unity of the sovereign and *Tawheed*, oneness or unity of God is the most important article of faith in Islam. The denial of this unity is the greatest conceivable violation of Islamic precepts (*Qur'an*, 2: 163, 6: 19, 16: 22, 23: 91-92, 37: 1-5, 38: 65-68, 112: 1-4). The sovereign by definition is universal as the Muslim community is seen as one *Ummah* (people) united under one sovereign by virtue of their faith and submission to the will of God. The word Islam means complete submission to God in the similar sense that the English philosopher Thomas Hobbes visualized the complete surrender of power by the individual to the state. The Islamic concept of submission is more powerful in that it subordinates human will to the will and law of God unconditionally. It is an ontological requirement and not a condition of any contract.

Thus to state succinctly, the Qur'anic concept of sovereignty is universal, that is nonterritorial, transcendental, meaning beyond human agency, indivisible, inalienable and truly absolute. God the sovereign is the primary lawgiver while agents such as the Islamic state and the Caliph enjoy marginal autonomy necessary to implement and enforce the laws of their sovereign. Man, as God's *Khalifa* on earth (vicegerent) is not only the primary agent of the sovereign but also enjoys a margin of autonomy. This margin of autonomy by virtue of vicegerency is the Islamic equivalent of popular sovereignty.

At a basic theoretical level the difference between the modern conception and Islamic conception of sovereignty is clear. The operational implications on closer examination seem to blur the distinction. The agency, or political action remains within human jurisdiction in either case. So whichever institution (form of government) is vested with the agency to act it either follows the *Shariah* (in the Islamic case) or the constitution in modern states. While constitutions can be amended the *Qur'an* is eternal, but it is open to different interpretations based on *ijtihad* or independent reasoning.

Maulana Maududi conceived of the term *Al-hakimiya*, a derivative of an Arabic word that means "to govern'". He introduced it in his work, *Al-Mustalahat al-Arba'a fi'l-Qur'an*. The term Al-hakimiya has been used by Islamic political thinkers ever since to mean sovereignty. He argued that according to Islam, sovereignty belonged to God. He alone was the lawgiver and that believers could neither resort to totally independent legislation, nor could they modify any law laid down by God. He saw the Islamic state as a political agency set up to enforce the laws of God. Herein lies the cardinal difference between the modern and Islamic conceptions. While modernity made the state a repository of sovereignty, in Islam the state was merely an agency of the sovereign. Thus the Islamic state is conceptually weaker than the modern state. Maududi also recognized the vicegerency of man and explained that each believer was a repository of the *Khalifah* (vicegerency). The *Qur'an* makes this explicitly clear (45: 12, 13). Maududi's understanding of the *Khalifah* of Man is definitely in the popular sense but he does not explain it in conjunction with sovereignty. Thus sovereignty lies in God, state is an agency of the sovereign and every believer is God's vicegerent on Earth. This however means that both the state and believers can legitimately act on behalf of the sovereign. Thus in Maududi's interpretation the sovereign has created dual agency in the Islamic state and the *Khalifah*, creating a balance or division of power between state and society. This mechanism can help ensure that both state and society follow the straight path.

The rise of political Islam has made the concept of Islamic sovereignty central to Islamic political theory and often it is presented as a barrier to any form of democracy. Democracies are seen as a system where human whim is the source of law where as Islamic principles are transcendental and cannot be undermined by popular whim. Unfortunately, what many of the Islamists fail to understand is that democratic institutions are not just about law. They are also about prevention of tyranny by the state. Regardless of where sovereignty is placed theoretically, in practice it is the state that exercises sovereignty in the world and not God or his angels.

These Islamists also fail to see that Muslims can actually enjoy greater autonomy in the imaginary Islamic state being discussed here, than even the citizens of a democracy like the U.S.. It is almost impossible to change or alter the American constitution. It would require an enormous amount of consensus in the society to make even a minor change. However, Islamic scholars have enjoyed a great deal of freedom, both politically and traditionally, to reinterpret the *Qur'an*

and Islamic principles. While in the U.S. people with different understanding of the constitution are not free to act legally according to
their own interpretation, Muslims have done precisely that and
legitimately. The presence of the various *madhahib* is a concrete
proof that a constitution/*Shariah* can be interpreted differently and
practiced accordingly

Sovereignty is a complex concept and any attempt to simplify it
can only cause problems. Nevertheless, Muslims must understand
that while sovereignty belongs to God it has already been delegated in
the form of human agency (*Qur'an* 2:30). The political task at the
moment is not to indulge in rhetoric that merely emphasizes this
point, but to reflect on how this God given agency can be best
employed in creating a society that will bring welfare and goodness to
people in the here and in the hereafter.

Muslims as individuals and as an *Ummah* cannot be held accountable for what they do unless they have the freedom/agency/sover-
eignty to do as they please. The discretion and the judgment with
which Muslims apply the given law not just to apply it but also to
achieve its *maqasid* (purpose) constitutes human sovereignty. The
Day of Judgment is the natural consequence of human sovereignty;
there cannot be one without the other. Therefore we must remember
that the freedom to act, human agency, is the most precious of gifts.
But it will have to be accounted for in full. So while we recognize
God's sovereignty in all affairs, he has exercised his sovereignty in
delegating some of it in the form of human agency. Having said that
I must also add that the slogan God alone is Sovereign cannot
become an excuse for installing and legitimizing governments that are
not accountable and responsible to their citizens.

Sources of Good Governance

*Those who, if We give them power in the land, establish
worship and pay the poor-due and enjoin kindness and
forbid iniquity. – Qur'an 22: 41* [Pickthall]

For centuries the quest for the formula of a just society and a
just state has preoccupied philosophers, theologians and political thinkers. The modern breed of political scientists has long given

up the search for justice and now merely occupies itself with running regression models about mundane issues.

Nevertheless, justice or no justice, in all eras, the dominant concern of all thinkers has been the search for institutions, blueprints or ideologies that would facilitate good governance.

In pre-modern times, political thinkers were not as concerned with the nature of the state as they were with the character of the ruler and that of the citizens. Political culture of nearly all societies was deeply influenced by religious mores and the definitions of good society, good ruler, and even the idea of "Good" itself was a religious derivative. God and Good were synonymous. Thus a good governor would inevitably need a legitimate association with God and hence the emergence and widespread propagation of the myth that rulers ruled with a divine mandate.

Whether it was the Japanese emperor, or the Chinese emperor, the Indian Raja or the European King, The Islamic Caliph or the Persian or Greek Ruler, all derived their legitimacy as well as agency from God explicitly. They were either supposedly ordained by God as sovereign rulers over their peoples or ruled on behalf of God. In some cultures, the difference between God and King often became unclear and the masses were encouraged to confuse the two. It was not just the Egyptian Pharaohs who claimed their Godhood, even Indian kings and Chinese emperors began to believe in their own divinity.

Because their "source" was legitimate, there was no need to judge the outcome of their rule. Thus regardless of whether they were able to provide just/good governance, these divinely ordained rulers were able to sustain their legitimacy and any attempt to examine their rule critically was as good as blasphemy. Even though, Islam has the concept of Good/God-given Laws (*Shariah*), after its initial explosion, Islamic society too began to implement the Good Men model as Sultans and Kings took titles such as *Zille-ilahi* (shadow of God) to legitimize their rule. It was not public welfare but the legitimacy of the ruler that determined continuity and loyalty.

The connection between individual virtue and good governance was widely assumed in premodern times. All major religions in the East, Confucianism, Buddhism, Hinduism and Islam advocated the following principles for establishing a good and just society. They preached that a good society was composed of "virtuous citizens" and ruled by "just and virtuous rulers". The entire focus of the educational apparatus was towards raising a virtuous elite that would govern justly and a virtuous citizenry that would remain loyal. The incentive/motivation for the pursuit of virtue was once again derived from a divine mandate. This epistemological-theological synthesis maintained that "since the nature of the unit determined the nature of the whole" politics was not "state-craft' but "soul-craft". Therefore the central themes of societal discourses were *Dao* (the universal path) in China, *Dharma* (duty/faith) for the Buddhist, *Karma* (deed/duty) for the Hindus, and *Aamal* (deeds/duties) for Muslims. For all these traditions, individual good results in social justice and harmony and *vice-versa*.

The modern era, with its secularism and the public private divide, breaks sharply from the past. Individual virtue and social structures are delinked. The assumption that in order to have a just society we necessarily need virtuous citizens and virtuous rulers is no more held as a self-evident truth. On the contrary the focus has shifted to "structures" and "constitutions". It is the law that now guarantees freedom and "equalitarianism". There is no more need for good men if there are good laws.

The growth of secular ideologies has continuously marginalized religion and religious virtue to a newly defined political quarantine called -- private space. Even though it is acceptable for homosexuals, gays, lesbians and feminists to politicize the private, for advocates of personal morality the public sphere is shrinking and increasingly the political is privatized. It is ironic that in an era when the state legislates about what happens in wombs and bedrooms, it still upholds a realm called private and confines virtue to it. The growth in crime, particularly crime and homicides by children; the growth in sexual abuse, rapes and molestations, and continuous decline in the moral health of society (I am assuming that the phrase moral health of society is still intelligible to many), are all indications of how we can have good laws without having good citizens.

American society, dominated by liberal inclination, has developed a predisposition towards blaming "structures" for moral failures. Indeed every instance of moral misconduct, whether by the President or by a serial killer is understood in the context of social structures that shaped that action. A hilarious example was Hillary Clinton's attempt to explain Bill Clinton's promiscuity on the "environment" in which he grew up. Childhood experiences or past social injustices have become a staple explanation for behavior that manifests any disregard for responsibility or moral consideration. Ethics is increasingly confused with political correctness and popularity not righteousness has become the criteria for evaluating conduct. This is not an occasion to critique liberal aberrations; it is enough to point out that the dangers of ignoring individual responsibility to emphasize structural obligations is systematically eroding the moral fabric of American society. Oklahoma, Columbine, Waco, Enron are but a few examples of where America is heading.

While the model of Good Men lead to Good societies undermines public accountability because the so called good men begin to take their legitimacy and their virtue for granted, the Good Laws lead to Good society model too is inadequate. It makes social structure an excuse for lack of personal responsibility. As a constructivist, one who believes that social reality is a joint outcome of individual action and social structural limitations, I tend to disagree with both models. We cannot have one without the other. As the traditional Islamic political theorists have maintained, a good society needs both good laws (in this case *Shariah* the divine constitution) and good men, (*Khulafa*, those who take accountability seriously).

The search for good governance may well include a search for a good constitution but it should not end there. It must also be accompanied by a search for the good citizen. It is only when good men find good laws that good societies emerge. Therefore the two quests must go hand-in-hand. While the postcolonial world searches for a "system" that will suit its indigenous needs and facilitate good governance, the democratic West should not celebrate the end of history and rest on its laurels. Even if it thinks that "democracy" is the best system it should still continue its quest for the good citizen.

What is Independent Thinking?

Speak up for justice; even if it means going against your own. – Qur'an 4: 135

When one exerts oneself (intellectually) and reaches the right conclusion one will get a double reward, but if one errs and makes a wrong judgment, one will still merit a reward.
– Abu Dawud (*Hadith* 3567)

A truly free and democratic society cannot be established until there are a large number of citizens willing and unafraid to think freely and independently. Independent thinking is not just a fruit of democracy; it is also the root of democracy.

For various theological and historical reasons the idea of "independent thinking" has become a highly contested one within the Muslim community. The term means different things to different people and based on these different understandings, people engage in either advocating or rejecting independent thinking among Muslims. In this article I hope to clarify some of the major interpretations of the term and the related politics of meanings.

The jurists use independent thinking as an elucidatory instrument. It is to be invoked in order to understand the injunctions of the *Shariah* on issues on which the primary sources, The *Qur'an* and the *Sunnah* are silent. For some it is an exercise of opinion (*Ra'y* as with the Hanafis) and for some it is merely the practice of *qiyas*, analogical reasoning (The Shafiis). There are of course some schools, which leave no room for any independent thinking claiming that the sources are comprehensive. There are also variations in this school of thought. Some privilege only The *Qur'an*, others overemphasize the *Sunnah*, and some claim to maintain a balance. The juristic understanding remains, conservative, often defensive and even paranoid.

Outside the discourse of the traditional jurists, intellectuals, reformers and philosophers, have seen independent thinking as not only inevitable but a mandate, that enables the continuous renewal and revival of the Islamic spirit. For them independent thinking is the use of reason, science, and experience to understand Islam in the present context and also understand God's creation. God has spoken to humanity through many media, texts and prophesy are just one medium. The universe around us is also God's continuous communication. Independent thinking is thus another way to understand God's message through reading his other book – nature. Ibn Tufayl's famous story of *Hai Ibn Yaqzan* is a brilliant example. In this novel Ibn Tufayl tries to show how Truth (including religious principles) can be discovered through reason.

To my mind, independent thinking is more than a "process" or an activity. It is also not just a juristic tool. For me independent thinking is a state of being. It is the state in which a human being realizes that he/she is a fully functioning cognitive, rational and moral being, aware that one is accountable for one's actions to a higher being, and would therefore like to always act intentionally and meaningfully. This intent and meaning in action can only come from within.

Therefore a comprehension and awareness of the logic and motivation behind every action is necessary. Such cognitive and reflective beings can only emerge if one takes one's cognitive and rational faculties seriously. If however one rejects one's own rational and cognitive capabilities then one has rejected one's own humanity. One can then only be an ape! Islamic theology has a term for this aping, it is called *taqleed*. I cannot conceive of any human and any Muslim as an ape. Therefore aping (taqleed) is not an option.

Given this, how do we understand the relationship between *Sunnah* and independent thinking? Does independent thinking necessarily reject *Sunnah*. NO! Independent thinking rejects aping, blind imitation, without understanding. Muslims are not required to blindly imitate the Prophet, we follow his example. For example, we choose to sport a beard even when safety razors are available but not ride a camel when a car is available. We understand the *Sunnah* and it's meaning so that when we act, we can also invest an Islamic meaning in our actions.

There are also popular understandings of the term independent thinking. Muslims, who believe that Islam is not limited to that past and its principles are adaptable to the changing conditions of modern life, see independent thinking as a means of reconciling the demands of contemporary life with Islamic injunctions.

But there are also Muslims, who are paranoid and think that independent thinking and *Shariah* are mutually exclusive. Therefore if we advocate independent thinking we advocate a departure from the *Shariah*. These Muslims are laboring under the assumption that the *Shariah* is a static body of *fiqh* articulated in the first and the second century of Islam. To put it bluntly, they confuse the opinions of the classical scholars with *Shariah* and so independent thinking becomes anti-*Shariah* because it may entail disagreements with past scholars.

Needless to say, the popular understanding of the term independent thinking is simplistic and over generalized. It is a mere reflection of people's attitude towards life itself. Those who are not afraid of change view independent thinking positively. While those who are afraid of change see independent thinking as dangerous, even anti-Islamic.

I believe that the present socio-political, economic, geopolitical, moral and cultural condition of the *Ummah* is less than acceptable. We cannot and must not exist as we do today. Therefore change is necessary, indeed inevitable. By corollary independent thinking is necessary and inevitable. It has to happen and will happen. It is only a matter of choice. Do we take the first step or wait for the next generation. Why put off until tomorrow what can be done now!

The Need for an 'Attentive Muslim Audience'

If only there had been among the generations before you men possessing a remnant (of good sense) to warn (their people) from corruption in the earth, as did a few of those whom we saved from them! – Qur'an 11: 116

For analytical purposes societies are often divided into two segments, the elites and the masses. However in contemporary developed societies, especially in democratic and reasonably free societies, it is more useful to include a third analytical category of the "attentive audience." The elite class consists of three types of elite – the normative, the political and the economic elite. In Western societies the normative class primarily consists of intellectuals, social scientists, social and political critics and journalists. This group, which can roughly be called the "brains" of the society, is responsible for developing an ideology that guides the state and guards the social and moral foundations of the society. They are the "meaning givers" who play a significant role in the legitimization process of dominant ideology and the regime in power.

The stability of societies is increasingly contingent on the degree of consensus that exists between the three elite groups. Once they agree upon the basic ideological character of the state, they establish mutually beneficial relationships, which often lead to enduring hegemony. The normative elite legitimize the coalition by providing intellectual and moral justifications and their authority is often enough to convince the masses. The political elite empowers and protects the interests and positions of the other two classes. The economic elite ensures that politicians and intellectuals are well rewarded for their efforts.

In the Muslim world, historically, the *Ulema* have monopolized the normative role. For brief periods they were challenged by the philosophers and the Sufi masters; but those moments were exceptions rather than the norm. Today one has seen the emergence of Islamists and secular intellectuals who have mounted a significant challenge to the traditional *Ulema* monopoly on the cognitive processes of the Muslim world. In America, the normative elite consists of the leadership of various Muslim organizations and associations such as ISNA, ICNA, IANA, and Muslim institutions such as AMC, IIIT and CAIR. They share this cell with the imported members of the *Ulema* from the Muslim world.

The Muslim masses, as is the case in most societies, remain ill informed and preoccupied with the mundane issues of existence. They often are victims of the authority of the normative elite, the power of the political elite and most likely are exploited by the economic elite. However the spread of education, information and the growth of the public sphere in the West, has led to the emergence of a highly sophisticated "attentive audience," a kind of cognitive middle class that shares the sophistication of the elite and the insecurity of the masses. But unlike the masses they are not an easy prey to the shenanigans of the ruling elite and are often capable of seeing through the false legitimacy that the normative elite provides to the dominant coalition.

By sharing the interest of the masses to maintain the balance of power between state and society, and being capable of discursively engaging the elite, the attentive audience begins to play the role of the society's conscience. In the absence of a critical cognitive elite that could check the cooption of the normative elite by the state, an attentive audience can play a significant role in preventing the emergence of authoritarianism or corporatism. They are mature citizens who understand the dynamics of power, are aware of the interests of the public, are cognizant of the potential for corruption in the higher echelons and are willing to participate in political or policy matters. It is their attentive and active participation that keeps the elite in check.

Muslims in America are badly in need of a healthy and active social conscience. We have no political elite and therefore the top layer is essentially a partnership between the interpreters and teachers of Islam and the rich – usually doctors and businessmen. They are the ones who make donations to the mosques and the ones who man the mosques. Muslims are further confounded by a lack of cohesion and consensus in the elite core, therefore we have a debilitating and often counter productive competition between various sets of elite coalitions that seek to win the allegiance of Muslim masses. The masses, often unable to understand the interests and the design of these various competing combinations, remain in disarray and confusion regarding what path to take, whom to trust and whom to pay their loyalties and their dues.

If Muslims can produce an attentive audience, then the interests of the community will be determined by a much larger community, not all members of which would be seeking leadership positions. This would also increase the discursive space that is common to the masses and the elite. Such a development would elevate the average maturity of the masses and make the elite, particularly the normative elite more responsible and grounded in reality and conscientious. Such a class of attentive audience members can emerge only through a systematic attempt to educate members of the public about issues of the day and getting them involved in thinking about shaping the future of the community. While the onus of education lies on the normative elite, the members of the public must realize that their leaders will serve them better, if they are better informed and more involved.

Peace, Justice and Change in Islam

And Allah summons to the abode of peace,
and leads whom He wills to the straight path.
– Qur'an 10: 25

That change is necessary in the Muslim World, both political and socio-cultural, is an eminently uncontested feeling. The issue that public intellectuals and policy makers must contemplate is whether this change can be engineered peacefully or will it have to be violent. Before we can reflect on any substantive issues regarding the impulse for change and the form this change will take, we must examine the idea of peace and nonviolence itself. What is the intrinsic value of peace and nonviolence? Are they to be valued in themselves to such an extent that the fear of violence and instability in the process of change compel us to indefinitely defer change?

Privileging peace and nonviolence as desirable values with intrinsic and not instrumental worth inevitably leads to the politics of status quo. If existing power regimes and ruling coalitions are not willing to relinquish power even in the face of popular opposition like in Algeria, then privileging of peace and stability becomes a defense of status quo even in the absence of legitimacy. However, the need for change should not be taken as a license to resort to violence in the face of political frustration.

If peace and nonviolence are to be conceived as instrumental values then there must be clearly identifiable values whose intrinsic worth must be more than that of peace. It is only when such values are identified that peace can be compromised in pursuit of these values which are more precious than peace itself. I wonder how many would challenge my contention that justice, equality and freedom are values more valuable than peace? I am not willing to give up my freedom or allow myself to be treated as an inferior or be treated unjustly without a fight. Can we demand people to give up their rights, freedom and accept injustices in the interest of maintaining peace?

Certainly not! But we can appeal to the oppressed and the downtrodden to give "peaceful change" a chance. We can defend instrumental peace and not peace as an inherent value worth achieving above everything else. Particularly with respect to a region where change is necessary, the engineering of peaceful, gradual and systematic change will preclude violent and revolutionary transformations.

The Qur'an offers a very sophisticated view of peace. In many verses it promises the believer peace as a final reward for a righteous life (5: 16). It also describes the house of Islam as the abode of peace (10: 25). At the behest of the *Qur'an*, Muslims greet each other every time they meet, by wishing peace for each other (6: 54). However the *Qur'an* does not shy from advocating military action in the face of persecution and religious intolerance. The strongest statement is in the Surah *al-Baqarah* (191):

And slay them wherever you find them, and drive them out of the places from where they drove you out, for persecution is worse than slaughter.

The presence of this verse in the *Qur'an* clearly precludes a complete prohibition of violence. The verse is important because in spite of the enormous significance that the *Qur'an* attaches to peace and harmony, it is categorical in its assertion that persecution is worse than killing. There is nothing allegorical in this verse it is clear: persecution is worse than killing (*Al-Qur'an*; 2: 217). Elsewhere the Qur'an states: *And fight them until persecution is no more* (8: 39). The Qur'anic preference for struggle against persecution and its promise to reward those who struggle in the path of Allah (4: 74) means that the only way violence can be eliminated from the Muslim World is by eliminating injustices and persecution. At the risk of sounding tautological one is back at square one, in order that there be peace, there must be change, can this change be peaceful? Perhaps we can minimize areas where violence can be used.

In al-Baqarah, The Qur'an says: *And fight them until persecution is no more, and religion is for Allah. But if they desist, then let there be no hostility except against wrong-doers* (2: 193). This verse is very interesting for it limits retaliation against all except those who are directly responsible for wrongdoing and also suggests that persecution could mean religious persecution. Meaning that when the practice of Islam is prohibited it is a condition that can be deemed as persecution and therefore fighting this persecution is desired. This could have implications for conflicts among Muslim states and between Muslim states and Islamic groups. Where citizens are allowed to practice their faith freely violence is not an option.

The *Qur'an* makes a profound pronouncement in al-Anfal: Tell those who disbelieve that if they cease (from persecution of believers) that which is past will be forgiven them (8: 38); this injunction further reduces the scope for violent response against persecution by granting amnesty to those who stop persecution. One of the reasons why tyrannical regimes persist in the Muslim World is due to the fear of retaliation. Regimes are resisting change and democratization for fear of being persecuted for past crimes by new regimes. A promise of general amnesty for past deeds by potential challengers may create an atmosphere where existing regimes may permit gradual change.

Thus philosophically speaking, we may not be able to completely eliminate the revolutionary option for instituting change, but there is enough meat in the *Qur'an* to limit violent response to egregious cases of religious persecution and repression.

Chapter 7

Attack on America and the Aftermath

Implications for Muslims Everywhere

He who has killed one innocent soul,
it is as if he has killed all humanity.
And he who has saved one soul,
is as if he has saved all humanity. – Qur'an 5: 32

What happened on September 11 is catastrophic. It is even bigger than Pearl Harbor. Words cannot describe the magnitude of the human tragedy that has taken place. The consequences of this event will be far reaching and will necessarily have global as well as local impact on Muslims.

Because the perpetrators of this extremely horrible, senseless and inhuman act were Muslims; decades of work by scholars, groups and activists, to improve relations between the U.S. and the Muslim World and their struggle to fight the negative image of Islam in the West, has been severely reversed.

The American response to the terrible tragedies will have an impact on U.S. role in world politics. Already domestic laws have transformed the civil rights environment of America. Legal standards protecting human rights and civil liberties have been lowered. Foreigners as well as citizens, particularly from the Arab and the Muslim World are all being treated as suspects.

Muslims in America are now at the mercy of the wisdom of American leadership. Many are being held for minor Visa violations, others are being interviewed leading to stigmatization. Muslims are now losing business and many have lost their jobs. The environment of suspicion is taking a heavy toll on innocent Muslims whose quality of life has taken a nosedive after September 11. The establishment must resist the impulse to solve investigative challenges by eliminating constitutional protections against abuse of power by the state. Doing so, would mean that the terrorists have succeeded in destroying the American way of life, and that would be their greatest victory.

This event will eventually strengthen the U.S. both internally and externally. More and more countries traditionally aligned against the U.S., like India, Russia and China will enhance their cooperation with the U.S. to fight international terrorism, global militancy from non-state actors and other forms of non-state violence. The attacks have become a rallying point around which much of the world, including many Muslim states, is uniting with the U.S. to deal more aggressively with global terrorism and conflicts.

This attack against innocent Americans is not only a test of American resolve and power, but is also a test of the loyalties of American Muslims. Today American Muslims have to decide who they are and where their loyalties lie. Trivial debates about whether they are American Muslims or Muslim Americans will have to be settled immediately. You cannot enjoy American hospitality and secretly applaud cowardly attacks against Americans.

Not all Muslims are terrorists and Islam does not condone such inhuman acts. No one disputes that. We must not allow the terrorists under any circumstances to alter our values and our sense of fairness and justice. It violates all that Islam stands for and must be condemned without reservation, whatsoever.

Individuals and groups who commit such acts are not only the enemies of Islam (because they give it a bad name by calling it *jihad*) but are also the enemies of humanity. They have confessed their complete lack of compassion for and solidarity with the human society. There is no need to feel defensive about Islam. Sometimes Muslims in their zeal to protect Islam act injudiciously. And when they do so they not only undermine the image of Islam but also cause untold harm to many Muslims.

Understanding the Roots of Muslim Resentment

The attacks on the World Trade Center and the Pentagon have raised several questions about Islam and militant Muslims. The chief among them are, why are some Muslims so angry at the U.S.

that they would perpetrate such an inhuman act? An even more puzzling question is how could Islam or any religion be a source of motivation or justification for such a gruesome act?

Before we answer the above questions, it is important to clarify that in spite of its gross inhumanity, the attack on America is certainly not the most egregious of crimes against humanity. The Spanish inquisition, the holocaust, the genocide in Bosnia, the systematic elimination of the native American population, the ethnic cleansings in Africa, and Cambodia, and even the atrocities against the Bosnians are by sheer number of casualties much bigger crimes. One may also recall that in India nearly 50,000 Sikhs were slaughtered in less than a week as revenge for the assassination of Indira Gandhi in early 1980s. In March 2002, nearly three thousand Muslims were slaughtered; many of them were burnt alive, in the state of Gujarat in India. What happened in Gujarat was more devastating and an even greater tragedy given the fact that while American victims have America to turn to, Gujarat Muslims have no one to turn to. Their own government is their enemy. But the attacks on America, because they were against America have far more of a global impact.

Why are Muslims Angry at the U.S.?

There are several theories being advanced by various commentators explaining why Muslims generally hate the United States. The silliest of them is the one that the Bush administration and the conservative elements in America entertain. They insist that Bin Laden and other Islamic militants hate American because they hate American values of freedom and democracy. Nothing can be further from the truth. Indeed most Muslims are great admirers of democracy and freedom and insist that these values are not only consistent with Islam but were the bedrock of the glorious Islamic civilization. They point to the diversity, tolerance and harmony at the peak of Islamic civilization to substantiate their claims.

As Islamic awareness increases in postcolonial Muslim societies and Islamic activists try to rebuild their civilization they find that the economically motivated alliance between secular authoritarian regimes in the Muslim world and the West, in particular the U.S., is the biggest barrier to freedom, democracy and self determination. Turkey, Algeria, Saudi Arabia, Bahrain, Kuwait are just a few examples of states where non-democratic regimes thrive and repress popular movements with U.S./Western support.

In 1953 a CIA coup replaced the democratic government of Muhammad Mossadeq in Iran with a monarchy so that Iran could become a client serving U.S. interests in the Middle East. In Algeria the west financed and legitimized a military coup that prevented Islamists from coming to power after winning an election. In the 1960s, and again in 1990s Turkey forced Islamists out of power, even after they had won popular mandates, with the tacit support from the U.S.. There are also absolutely no examples to show that the U.S. has either supported or encouraged democratic reforms anywhere in the Muslim World.

The utter lack of peaceful channels for protest and dissent in the entire Arab world has slowly radicalized most moderate Islamic oppositions. The use of brutal force by secular regimes has further incited reactionary violence from Islamic militias. There is also a false notion circulating that Islam and democracy are incompatible. Today nearly 800 million Muslims live in democratic societies. As of now there are two Muslim nations with over a 100 million people that have women heads of state – Indonesia and Bangladesh. The U.S. has not had one in over 220 years!

It is not a hatred of democracy and freedom but the desire for one that has made many Muslims hate the U.S. whom they blame for the perpetuation of undemocratic polities in their world. Surely there are some Muslims who argue that democracy like everything Western is UnIslamic and evil. Fortunately such misguided people are few and have very little influence in the Muslim World.

Many Muslims also believe that the U.S. is inherently opposed to Islam and Muslims. Bin Laden for one has claimed that by maintaining troops in Saudi Arabia (to protect the monarchy from any popular revolutions) the U.S. actually occupies the two most important Muslim holy sites, Makkah and Madina. And through Israel, which is seen as an outpost of Western imperialism in the Arab world, the U.S. occupies Jerusalem the third most holy Muslim city.

Add to this the systematic destruction of Iraq, the death of over a million Iraqi children through U.S. sponsored sanctions, and the daily atrocities, assassinations and dispossession of the Palestinians by a U.S. armed and funded Israeli army, it is not difficult to imagine why U.S. is not seen as a beacon of freedom and virtue in the Muslim World.

Does this mean that angry Muslims are allowed to perpetrate collateral damages that include over 3000 innocent Americans? Certainly not. The purpose of this article is not to condone what happened on September 11. What happened was horrible, inhuman and unIslamic. But reflection over Muslim grievances can help us understand how even devout people can be driven to commit themselves to terror. Systematic repression dispossesses people of their humanity, inciting them to commit inhuman acts.

How Can Islam permit/incite terror?

Any observer of the Palestinian problem, who does not nurse malice towards Islam, will understand why many Palestinians would resort to terrorism and suicide bombings against Israel. Surely, if we were to equip them with F-16s and Apache helicopters they would also fight fair and square with Israel. As far as killing of innocent civilians is concerned, the Israeli army kills many times more Palestinian children than the casualties caused by suicide bombers. Islam is merely used by Hamas and Islamic Jihad as a rhetorical instrument for mobilization of resistance. The important point is that it is not the Islamic belief of Palestinians that leads them to suicide bombing but rather the logic of the circle of violence in that conflict. Also remember that Japanese pilots in World War II and Tamil Elam Tigers (of Buddhist and Hindu religions) have used suicide bombing more often than Muslims. Long before Hamas emerged, a suicide bomber had assassinated Rajiv Gandhi, India's Prime Minister.

Islam is the most practical, rational and realistic of all religions. It is this realistic element in Islam that does not fully advocate pacifism, permitting the use of force. The theory of *Jihad* (Struggle in the path of God) forbids violence except when (1) Muslims are not allowed to practice their faith (freedom of religion is threatened) (2) when people are oppressed and subjugated (in pursuit of freedom) and (3) when people's land is forcibly taken from them.

Islam allows a range of responses. One can forgive the oppressor or one can respond in kind. There are Qur'anic sources encouraging both positions.

> *And slay them wherever you find them, and drive them out of the places from where they drove you out, for persecution is worse than killing* (2: 191).

> *Tell those who disbelieve that if they cease persecution of believers that which is past will be forgiven them.* (8: 38)

There is no hierarchy of verses in the *Qur'an*. Those who privilege the first verse over the second will wage war to fight injustice. And most militant Muslims invoke this verse in the defense of their actions. But then there are Muslims who privilege the second verse and seek diplomatic end to persecution through forgiveness. The two verses above are exemplary of the tension between realism and idealism in Islam. But in the final analysis Islam is what Muslims make of it.

While war in search of justice and to escape persecution is permissible in Islam, what happened on September 11 certainly is not. I wonder how those Muslims responsible for the slaughter of American civilians would rationalize their actions in the light of this Qur'anic verse:

> *He who has killed one innocent soul, it is as if he has killed all humanity. And he who has saved one soul, is as if he has saved all humanity* (5: 32).

The Saga of Osama Bin Laden

Do no mischief on earth. – Qur'an 7: 56, 7: 74

B in Laden has become a significant moral challenge to Muslims. His association with the perpetrators of September 11 attacks raises a major question about the relationship between Islam and terrorism. If he is guilty then he incriminates the faith of Islam by using it as a motivation and justification for his actions. If he is innocent, then why is he such a big hero?

If Bin Laden is not guilty of the embassy bombings, of the attack on USS Cole and the attack on America then why do some Muslims admire him? Bin Laden has become a symbol of resistance and empowerment to a community deprived of freedom and opportunities for self-determination. He is a hero to a community that has long got used to living with an overwhelming sense of helplessness. He is a promise that even the weak and the hopeless can strike back.

If my understanding of why Bin Laden is a hero is correct then it means that his charisma is dependent on Muslim acceptance that he is indeed responsible for the various attacks against the U.S., regardless of the availability of evidence. He is a hero because some Muslims believe that he indeed pulled of all those spectacular attacks against the world's sole superpower. His heroism and his popularity in the Muslim world is an indictment of him as a terrorist and his supporters as supporters of terrorism.

But Muslims, without any reservations, have condemned the attacks of September 11 as morally reprehensible and unjustifiable. Prominent member of the Ulema have also established the unIslamic character of the September 11 attacks. All Muslims agree that terrorism is unIslamic and deplorable and the perpetrators must be punished to the fullest extent of the law.

Bin Laden has denied any connections to the attacks and many Muslims believe that he is really innocent and are critical of the American establishment for not providing conclusive evidence against Bin Laden before launching a war against Afghanistan. But even while denying the attacks, he has repeatedly said he supports the attacks and has also justified the choice of targets and the deaths of innocent Americans in a lengthy interview to a Pakistani journalist.

Moreover a videotape which was found in a house in Jalalabad was released by the Pentagon and for many this tape erases any doubts about Bin Laden's involvement in the September 11 attacks on America. Prominent American Muslim organizations like the Council on American and Islamic Relations (CAIR) have come out stating that there can be no more doubts about Bin Laden's involvement in the dastardly attacks. CAIR also expressed its horror at Bin Laden's comment that the act itself had benefited Islam.

The tape is probably better than anything that the American administration could have wished for. It not only indicates that Bin Laden had intimate knowledge about the planning of the attacks, but was also more aware of the details than the actual perpetrators themselves. The tape clearly suggests Bin Laden's role as the mastermind behind the attacks. The tapes also give an insight into the moral character of Bin Laden. His callous attitude towards innocent casualties is appalling. How can someone claim to be a devout Muslim and yet be so insensitive to human pain and suffering?

One of the most disturbing elements of the Bin Laden phenomenon was his popularity among disenfranchised Muslims. He was using just causes to justify unjust methods and was systematically corrupting the interpretation of Islamic ideals such as *adl* (justice) and *jihad* (just struggle). He was glamorizing terrorism and was clearly a disastrous role model for Muslim youth in search of dignity and social justice.

Bin Laden's use of the concept of *Jihad* is false and is a gross misinterpretation of Islam. *Jihad* is not a war by any means against unbelievers. The theory of *Jihad* (Struggle in the path of God) forbids violence except when (1) Muslims are not allowed to practice their faith (freedom of religion is threatened) (2) when people are oppressed and subjugated (in pursuit of freedom) and (3) when people's land is forcibly taken from them. Islam specifically forbids suicide (*Qur'an* 4: 29) and the killing of civilians, women and children (Bukhari: *Book of Jihad*).

Moreover the *Qur'an* forbids *fitnah* (mischief; 7: 56, 7: 74) and the classical Islamic jurists have clearly argued that *Hirabah* (terrorism or war against society) is strictly unIslamic and forbidden.

There is more than enough evidence in Islamic sources to expose the fundamentally erroneous nature of Bin Laden's theology.

Hopefully this tape and the subsequently gathered evidence will achieve two desirable objectives. One, it will convince most of the doubters about Bin Laden's guilt. Two, it will give pause to the supporters of Bin Laden and they will realize the gravity and inhumanity of his methods. One cannot indulge in such enormously devastating attacks without allowing the kernel of morality, goodness and humanity within oneself to die. I hope and pray that no one else follows in the footsteps of Bin Laden.

There will still be those who will deny the evidence the tape advances. They will probably claim that for those who could orchestrate an attack like the one on September 11, it will be a small matter to produce a tape like this one using a Bin Laden look alike and poor quality video and audio. It may also lead to an entire industry of conspiracy theories seeking to explain away the tape. We can only sympathize with such naiveté. In a sense such extreme denial is indicative of the people's belief that no Muslim could commit such a horrible attack, especially in the name of Islam.

The saga of Bin Laden is a wakeup call to the U.S. and the Muslim World. We must never forget that the U.S. had a role in the very creation of Bin Laden and his types. Bin Laden is the real face of the mythical Rambo who was created to terrorize and destroy the Soviets. Americans used Bin Laden and his Afghan Arabs in the war against the Soviet Union, armed and trained them and then left them without demobilizing and resettling them. The U.S. must recognize that it cannot produce such lethal weapons and not one-day pay the price.

The analogy is similar to that of Hamas. The Israelis initially played a supportive role in the emergence of Hamas hoping they could bring about a rift between the Palestinians. Now like the U.S. they are themselves victims of the lethal weapons they helped produce.

Muslims everywhere, must realize that extremism among some Islamic activists, has indeed reached inhuman proportions. In the name of Islam and for the benefit of Islam, these extremists are prepared to commit murder and mayhem. It is absolutely imperative that Muslims who care about humanity in general and the image of Islam in particular, launch a campaign against extremism in the Muslim world. We have to become intolerant towards intolerance and give no quarter to any form of verbal, theological, or political extremism.

Bin Laden has left a horrible scar on Muslim history. We must work hard to erase it. We can do that by reviving the Qur'anic principles of *Ihsan* (moral excellence) and *Rahmah* (mercy/tolerance) in our social and political interactions within and without the Muslim world.

We Muslims have to realize that Bin Laden and his tactics, no matter how just his causes, are detrimental to Muslims as well as to the image of Islam.

Even if for the sake of argument we believe that Bin Laden has nothing to do with September 11; this man is still guilty of the following acts: He has blasphemed Islam. He has used its sacred principles to incite murder and mayhem. He has declared war on the U.S. and called on all Muslims to murder Americans making Muslims targets for retaliatory attacks. He has exposed millions of Afghans to war, starvation and misery to save his own skin. If he were a hero, he would have surrendered. Not because he was guilty, but to save poor innocent Muslims from the ravages of war.

He has attacked the moral fabric of Muslim life by glorifying terrorism. He is trying to embroil the Muslim *Ummah* in a global war of death and destruction by calling the American war on Bin Laden as a war on Islam. His use of Islamic values have made Muslims look like terrorists and in most parts of the world people are associating Islam with violence and Muslims with terror. Bin Laden and the extremist interpretation his types advocate is deeply detrimental to Islam and Muslims and must be resisted by all Muslims.

It is time Muslim scholars and leaders fulfilled their Islamic duty and rescued not only Islam but also our misguided youth from the clutches of the Bin Laden phenomenon.

The Domestic Dimension of the Arab-Israeli Conflict

For decades pro-Israeli lobbyists have operated under the assumption that Islam and Israel are locked up in a zero-sum-game. They see the growth of Islam and growth of Islamic consciousness as a threat to the very existence of Israel. Based on this operating premise, pro-Israeli forces have sought to undermine the spread of Islam in the U.S. and stem the increasing political significance of American Muslim organizations. It is easy to understand the fears of the friends of Israel. In order to sustain Israel's military advantage over Arabs, they have to sustain the asymmetrical balance of power between American Jewish lobby and the American Muslim lobby.

In the post September 11 politics, this domestic and not so visible dimension of the Arab-Israeli conflict has become more and more hectic. This issue came in to public eye when some members of an extremist Jewish organization, the JDL (Jewish defense League) were arrested for plotting to blow up a Muslim mosque, the office of a Muslim organization and the offices of an Arab congressman from California.

While pro-Israeli Jewish organizations are flooding American media with information allegedly linking Muslim organizations with terrorists (often the tips come in the form of oral and written records of careless statements by Muslim leaders), Muslim organizations and activists are working feverishly to argue that terrorism is a consequence of Israeli atrocities against Palestinians and U.S. foreign policy in the Middle East. Some Muslims have even tried to plant the idea that Israelis may have committed the attacks of September 11.

This Muslim-Jewish byplay is not good for the social health of America and already long-standing Muslim-Jewish dialogues have suffered because of this rise in Muslim-Jewish tension. While Muslims definitely share responsibility for this state of affairs, a disproportionate amount of attacks are coming from the Jewish side. American Muslims are already besieged by the administration's treatment of American Muslims as suspects and the additional attacks from their cousins (Jews and Muslims are biblical cousins from the two sons of Prophet Abraham) are making things worse.

Perhaps the Bush administration already senses this as can be seen by Mrs. Cheney's comments at the Anti-Defamation League dinner in Chicago (Nov 12). She said, "Muslims should not be blamed "for the actions of a fanatic few." President Bush himself has condemned anti-Muslim and anti-Islamic xenophobia. The attacks on Islam however have continued unabated and it seems that there is a method behind this madness. The attacks seem to be systematic and at many levels.

The first major strike was launched by the American Jewish Committee (AJC), which published a study estimating American Muslim population to about 2.6 million. The general opinion is that there are between 6-7 million Muslims in America. AJC is concerned that over estimation of Muslim population is making American politicians and American media more sensitive to American Muslim concerns. The study is actually not even a real survey but a review article that merely studies other estimates and then advances its own guesstimate.

The timing of the report, after September 11, when the American Muslim community was already battered verbally and even in some cases physically by rising anti-Muslim sentiment, is indicative of the strategic animus behind the study. Imagine any other religious community, Catholics, Baptists, or Muslims conducting a survey of how many Jews really live in America. This would be immediately construed as anti-Semitic and there would be a huge uproar against such bigotry. But AJC has suffered no backlash from anyone in the media or the government.

Then there are attacks against American Muslim organizations and their leaders. Prominent spokespersons are Daniel Pipes of the Middle East Forum in Philadelphia, an openly pro-Israeli think tank and Steve Emerson a self styled "documentarian" of Muslim organizations; who have been trying to paint prominent Muslim organizations as terrorist organizations and Muslim leaders as sympathizers and supporters of terrorism. The objective is clear. By labeling prominent Muslim organizations as "connected with terror" and Muslim leaders as supportive of terrorism, Pipes et al are trying to disarm the community in its struggle against Islamophoebia. By undermining

Muslim organizations, they also hope to reduce Muslim access to the Congress and the White House.

In spite of several articles in the media and accusations on TV against American Muslim organizations and American Muslim leaders by Pipes and Emerson, and repeated investigations by the FBI, none has been indicted or arrested. American Muslim leaders and organizations' only failing is that they have not fully learned to play "American political games" skillfully. Sometimes their naiveté and even sincerity leads them to make strategic errors as they seek to balance their loyalties to America and to Muslims worldwide. Riding two horses is never too easy and sometimes, Muslim leaders do look ungainly. But that does not make them terrorists or traitors. If it is ok to be loyal to America and Israel, then it is ok to be loyal to America and the *Ummah*. Only American Muslims have to learn to be so with as much skill and finesse as displayed by pro-Israeli lobbies.

The most sophisticated version of the attack on Islam is the attempt to besmirch the reputation of prominent American scholars of Islam and the Middle East who advance different analysis of Islam and Islamic resurgence from that maintained by Israel. A recent book, *Ivory Towers on Sand: The Failure of Middle Eastern Studies in America* authored by an Israeli scholar, Martin Kramer, and published after September 11 by a pro-Israel think tank, The Washington Institute for Near East Policy, criticizes the entire academy. Interestingly this book is just another version of an article written by (no prizes for guessing) Daniel Pipes and De Atkine, Middle Eastern Studies: What went Wrong? in the Winter 1995-1996 issue of *Academic Questions*.

All these attacks by the Israeli lobby are designed to undermine and even rollback the growing influence of American Muslims.

But this is not the time for political intramurals. At present American leaders, American media, American Muslims and Jews, and all other Americans must rise above sectarian and special interests in order to help America recover from the aftermath of September 11, and devote their energies to guarantee American security, protect American freedoms, and revive American economy. Once we have the boat on an even keel, we can return to partisanship and bickering, after all they are also a quintessential part of the American way.

Islamic Movements:
The Missing Dimension in the War Against Terror

So far the fragile global alliance created by George Bush has survived a prolonged military operation in Afghanistan. But Afghanistan is only the first step in this terrible war on terror. The post Afghanistan aspects of this war are more complex and the enemy is also not easily identified. The second phase of this campaign will have to rely more heavily on accurate and timely intelligence and will entail covert operations in the territories of friendly nations. The second stage will require far more active and systematic cooperation from various elements of Muslim societies if the U.S. really seeks to eliminate all anti-U.S. militant organizations. Passive support from the so-called moderate and friendly regimes will not be enough. This campaign will also have to be accompanied with a more complex alliance building with various institutions within Muslim societies.

In assembling a global coalition to fight anti-U.S. terrorism, George Bush has so far ignored a powerful player with global reach – Islamic movements and their scholars. Even though terror and counter-terror is essentially a contest between states and non-state actors, Bush and his aides have until now only focused on rallying support from Muslim states and Islamic movements have not been approached. This oversight may prove to be expensive. Many regimes in the Muslim world, for example Turkey, Egypt, Algeria and Pakistan, are seen as secular and anti-Islamic. Allying with these states and not Islamists can easily be construed as an anti-Islamic move.

The administration must realize that there is a great diversity between Islamic associations. While all seek change and political reform, there is a significant difference in how they wish to Islamize their societies. There are moderate movements seeking to revive Islamic rituals like the *Tablighi Jamaat*, a global force, that is singularly focused on rituals and in many ways secularizes Islam because of its strong antipathy for political involvement. There are other revivalist movements like the *Ikhwan* (Muslim Brotherhood) in the Arab world and the *Jamaat-e-Islami* in South Asia.

For sure these movements are anti-Western in their rhetoric and are opposed to U.S. support for Israel and authoritarian regimes in the Middle East that suppress them. But these movements consider themselves as legitimate foundations of the Muslim civil society, seeking political and social reform (Islamization) primarily through *Dawa* – a peaceful and ritualistic call to Islam. They are not violent and have no desire to be associated with terror. Islamic movements such as *Al Nahda* in Tunisia and *Refah* in Turkey have never used violence as vehicle for change. Almost all of these movements support the call for a civilizational dialogue and have engaged in sustained inter-faith activities.

These movements seek authenticity and socio-political space to explore the worldly implication of being a Muslim. They are also determined to prove that Islam is the best way of life in order to attract new believers. Use of violence and association with terrorism, even remotely, fundamentally undermines their *raison d'etre*. Increasingly these movements are seeking Western support in the democratization of the Muslim World. Most of their leaders are western educated and some, like Rashid Ghannushi of *al Nahda* have openly expressed their admiration for democracy and its virtues in the West.

These movements would also like to join the coalition, for if they do not, the repressive regimes in the Muslim world may use this war on terrorism as a cover to eliminate them. These movements would like to the join the coalition, their rhetoric not withstanding, to gain global legitimacy and also protect themselves from the repressive policies of the regimes that keep them out of the political loop. These moderate movements, if included in the coalition can play a significant role in preventing the radicalization of millions of devoted mainstream Muslims. If excluded these movements will reposition the war on terrorism as a war on Islam in order to destabilize states such as Egypt, Pakistan and Saudi Arabia for a wholesale political transformation of the Muslim World.

These movements and the intellectuals and the scholars associated with them can become a great asset in the war against terror, if the Bush administration really means it when it claims that this is a war against terror and not Islam. There are at least two strategic reasons for seeking the cooperation of Islamic movements. To use Bush's own words, "If you are not with us, you are against us," implies that if Islamic movements are not included in the coalition then they will also become a target of the coalition. This is exactly the scenario that the U.S. claims it is seeking to avoid – a war against Islam. The present allies of the U.S. in the Arab world, the so-called moderate regimes represent neither Muslims nor Islam. It is the Islamic movements who enjoy popular franchise and they represent Islam as well as Muslims in most of the Middle East. Excluding them means excluding Islam and Muslims.

Unlike the revivalist movements, Islamic militias like Islamic Jihad, Hamas, Hezbollah, and Harakatul Mujahideen are committed to the use of political violence to realize their goals. These groups in self-defense will seek to interpret the war on their opposition to Israel and U.S. as a war on Islam to undermine the coalition and to gain more support from Muslims. The involvement of bigger and more mainstream Islamic movements in the coalition will minimize the extent to which these militias can use Islam.

By distinguishing between militias and movements and recruiting the cooperation and the goodwill of Islamic movements, the Bush administration can send the message across that this is not a war against Islam in truly meaningful terms. It will also give their actions some degree of legitimacy in the eyes of Muslims if prominent Islamic scholars and leaders of the Islamic movement endorse them.

In simple terms the Special Forces would go in after Bin Laden and his comrades armed with Fatwas that say that Islam forbids the killing of innocent citizens and condemns those who create mischief on Earth. There are several prominent Muslim scholars who have in recent days condemned the wanton massacre of innocent civilians in New York and Washington, DC. It will not be difficult to enlist their support and cooperation. They can and will become an important element of the coalition.

The Bush administration can do this by delegating the North American *Fiqh* Council and the *Shariah* Scholars Association to hold a world Islamic conference in Washington and invite the leaders of various Islamic movements to this conference to condemn terrorism. Right now, American Muslim scholars are falling over each other to condemn the attacks and distance Islam from the perpetrators of terror. They will be only too happy to hold such a conference.

Towards a New Ethic of Peace

We made you a nation of moderation and justice
– Qur'an 2: 143

To advocate what is right and forbid what is wrong
– Qur'an 3: 110

The war on terrorism is not likely to end quickly. Some elements in Washington, DC expect it to last a generation. As long as the cycle of terror and counter-terror continues, the relations between Islam and the West will remain strained and contentious. Muslims in the West will continue to find themselves in a precarious situation, oscillating between the two poles -- suspects and cultural bridges. Intellectuals, concerned citizens and political leaders in the West as well as in the Muslim World will have to fundamentally rethink their positions and strategies in order to escape a prolonged cycle of war and terror. Muslim intellectuals in the West will have to realize their potential to become cognitive bridges and advance new paradigms on the basis of which peace activists and cultural and community ambassadors can undermine and subvert the forces of war and terror.

There are three dangers against which all peace loving people must be on guard; (1) This conflict must not be allowed to become a clash of civilizations between Islam and the West/Rest. (2) Hawks and extremists must not be allowed to hijack and dominate the discourses in the West and in the Muslim World. (3) The search for security and revenge should not be allowed to undermine the moral fabric of our societies.

Defend Dissent and Difference in America

Hawks in the West who may entertain Islamphoebic sentiments must abstain from exhorting the American government to extend its military campaign to other Muslim nations.
Indiscriminate bombing will only lead to further anger and hatred
against the West and will incite more violence from militant Muslims.
Some of these hawks are now claiming "we are all Israelis". Implying
that since the U.S. has now also become a victim of political violence
of Muslim extremists, it is time the U.S. also responded in the same
way as Israel.

Americans must guard against such bad advice from those friends
of Israel who are pessimistic about the prospects of peace between
Israel and Palestine and would like nothing better but to get the U.S.
to do its dirty work; such as eliminating all Palestinian resistance to
Israel in the name of fighting terrorism. Heavy-handed military tactics
as displayed by Ariel Sharon's present tenure have done little to
enhance Israeli security but have plunged the nation into a never-
ending spiral of violence.

America does not wish to enter into a never-ending violence with
Muslims who number over 1.4 billion and live in nearly all nations of
the earth. Israeli military tactics have severely undermined its claims
to being the only democracy in the Middle East. Surely America
does not wish to destroy its own democracy to pursue Israeli interests.
Even though the new terrorism bill and the new executive order
permitting the use of military tribunals for trials and executions have
already jeopardized the Bill of Rights and pushed the U.S. down
several notches on the scale of democracy, it should not try to
become another Israel.

It is the responsibility of American media and American intellectuals and peace lovers to ensure that hawks and warmongers do not
monopolize the national agenda. So far American media has not
done justice to its role as the voice of the people and the conscience
of the government. By completely capitulating to the governmental
agenda they have become to the U.S. what Pravda use to be to the
USSR – state sponsored media.

Loud dissent and systematic criticism of the manner in which Bush administration is conducting this war on terrorism is absolutely necessary to ensure that excesses at home or abroad are not committed. The war against terror should not itself become terror at home or overseas. The moral responsibility of ensuring this lies with the political opposition, the media, the academics and public intellectuals and commentators. I hope that in the interests of American security and democracy, these voices will speak up and be heard.

Moderate voices in America must defend American democracy and resist that danger that hasty and undebated legislations and executive orders pose to the civil rights of minorities. A paranoid government should not be allowed to essentially rewrite the U.S. constitution. Moderate voices in America must also speak up and challenge the dangerous domination of misguided patriotism before the war on terror becomes a war on dissent and difference in America.

The dominant discourse in America is focusing on two issues – understanding Islam and building national unity. Both these themes are problematic. While there is a lot of positive reflection and discussion of Islam, the heightened interest in Islam inevitably stems from the fundamental assumption that somehow Islam is behind the horrible tragedies of September 11. This is not only a great insult to one of civilizations greatest heritage it is also strategically misleading. A better understanding of Islam, however desirable, will not lead to an understanding of why September 11 happened.

Americans may find more answers if they placed their foreign policy under the microscope. It is time they stopped obsessing over Bin Laden and Islam and examined the recent history of their actions overseas to grasp the depth of hatred they engender among foreigners. A quick look at the State department's annual report on terrorism will show that nearly 60% of all anti-U.S. terrorist acts happen in Latin America. Neither an absence of democracy or presence of Islam will explain why the democratic and UnIslamic Latin Americans hate the U.S..

In search of unity, American leaders are compromising the most important aspect of American society – freedom. It is time we realize that it is not insecurity but forced unity which is the biggest threat to freedom in America. Since September 11, I have spoken at many Universities across the nation, been on tons of radio and TV shows and written for nearly 100 different media outlets and I have noticed a huge difference in what is said in the media and what is said across campuses by professors as well as students. I know this for certain all Americans voices are not represented either in the media or in the government.

Students and academics all across America are not only critical of American foreign policy but also deeply afraid of the deterioration of the protection of civil liberties in America. Most of them wish to revamp old notions of national interest and advocate a more benign international outlook. Many are deeply disturbed by the violence the U.S. itself seems to be capable of. But sadly, many of them are afraid to speak out in public outside university campuses, or in the media. This fear, this insecurity, this loss of freedom is not because of the terrorist attacks of September 11, but because of the attacks on dissent and difference by the government and the media in the aftermath of September 11. It is not the terrorists, but our search for a national unity, which is destroying our freedoms.

Muslims Must Enjoin Moderation and Forbid Extremism

Muslim Moderates in the West as well as in the Muslim World must become aggressive in their dealings with the extremists in their midst. The first step is to recognize, that when moderates remain silent extremists speak for all. Those Muslims who do not wish to be represented by the likes of Osama Bin Laden must speak out loud and clear. They must let the world know in no uncertain terms that terrorists like Bin Laden do not represent them. What is also extremely crucial is that they reject specific interpretations of Islam and Islamic principles that people like Bin Laden use in order to justify murder and mayhem of innocent civilians, women and children.

If they choose to remain silent, for whatever purpose, then they must share the blame for the association of Islam with terrorism.

They must also not complain if the rest of the world mistakes their cowardly silence on terrorism as support for terrorism and terrorists. Moderate Muslims must also remember that vague and generalized statements condemning terrorism are not helpful. They must condemn specific acts and specific individuals and groups associated with those acts. If you are against terrorism then let the world know that in unequivocal terms.

Many Muslims, including some American Muslims have become hypocritical in our advocacy of human rights and in our struggles for justice. We protest against the discriminatory practices of Israel, India, and other non-Muslim nations; but are mostly silent against the discriminatory practices within Muslim states. We rightly condemn Israeli treatment of Palestinians at all international forums. But our silence at the way many Muslim nations have treated the same Palestinians really questions our commitment and concern for them. Isn't it a tragedy that in spite of all the Muslim support for Palestinians, more Western nations than Muslims nations allow them to become their citizens?

While we loudly and consistently condemn Israel for its ill treatment of Palestinians and Russian excesses in Chechnya or Serbia atrocities in Bosnia, we remain silent when Muslim regimes abuse the rights of Muslims and slaughter thousands of them. Where were we when Saddam used chemical weapons against Muslims (Kurds)? Or when the Pakistani army massacred Muslims (Bengalis)? When Syria massacred thousands of Islamists in Hama, did we launch a campaign against Syria? Have we demanded international intervention or retribution against Muslim nations that commit egregious violations of Muslim human rights? Is our lukewarm criticism of Muslim regimes the Islamic way? Are Muslims not supposed to stand for justice even if it meant taking a position against our own dear ones? (*Al Qur'an* 6: 152).

It is time that we faced these hypocritical practices and struggled to transcend them. For decades we have watched as Muslims in the name of Islam have committed violence against other Muslims from the Iran-Iraq war to the struggles in Afghanistan. As Muslims can we condone such inhuman and senseless waste of life in the name of Islam? The culture of hate and killing is tearing away at the moral fabric of the Muslim society. We are more focused on "the other" and have completely forgotten our duty to Allah. In pursuit of the inferior jihad we have sacrificed the superior *jihad*.

Today the century old Islamic revival is in jeopardy because we have allowed insanity to prevail over our better judgment. It is time we put an end to this madness. It is time that Muslim moderates rescued Islam and Muslim causes from the clutches of extremists. As I see it, the only way out is through an extreme intolerance for intolerance. Moderate Muslims must fight against all forms of prejudice, hatred and intolerance within Muslim ranks and militantly advocate peaceful resolutions of conflict within and without the community. Indeed Muslim moderates must wage *Jihad* (struggle) against *Hirabah* (Islamic legal term for war against society or terrorism) and realize the Qur'anic mandate that Muslims are a nation of moderation and justice (2: 143).

Privilege Morality over Strategy

There are two levels at which one can respond to any crisis; at the moral level and at the strategic level. Strategic responses are usually designed to prevent future crisis, minimize present damage and also provide an explanation of what happened, and how it happened. Strategic responses are often based on technological premises and guided by the amorality of realpolitik. Moral responses on the other hand seek an understanding of what happened and deal with the issue from a humanist perspective.

Both the West and the Muslim World have responded to the attacks of September 11 from a strategic perspective. Without really caring for what has motivated such extreme actions against the U.S., the U.S. and its allies have launched a series of strategic and technical campaigns designed towards diminishing the capacity of potential attackers and their allies. The Muslim world has also responded strategically. Muslim states have moved with incredible haste to safeguard their national/regime interests while Muslim civil society, particularly in the West, has geared up to defend itself as if it were involved in a war between Islam and the west.

The dangers of strategic responses and realpolitik thinking are that they marginalize morality and in my mind, our morality is our humanity. If we put aside our morality we will indulge in inhuman acts. When strategic discourse become dominant, the principle of reciprocity becomes the overriding concern. Tit for tat, an eye for an eye becomes the order of the day. Terror and counter-terror becomes a way of life. The recent state of life in Palestine and Israel since October 2000 is a good example of the degeneration of order and quality of life when strategic thinking consumes everyone.

From an Islamic standpoint, the domination of strategic thinking and the principle of reciprocity are unacceptable. Muslims are supposed to be a moral community whose Islamic mandate is to enjoin good and forbid evil. The objectives of the Islamic way are to establish a just society and an environment that facilitates the perfection of the soul. A strategic environment is detrimental to the moral health of the individual soul as well as the social fabric of the society.

When society is gripped in a strategic struggle and reciprocity becomes the overriding principle, the humanity of the self becomes contingent on the humanity of the other. If we allow our actions and our responses to be dictated by the actions of others, then both self and the other, mirror each other. We will remain human only if the other chooses to remain human. It is indeed ironic that we allow our humanity to be dictated by the choices of our enemies.

When the U.S. responds to the murder of innocent people with massive attacks that kills more innocent people, then it is merely responding to terror with terror. When Islamic scholars claim that suicide bombings against Israel are permissible because the Israeli army also kills civilians and children, then they have conceded the interpretation of Islamic law to the Israeli army. Regardless of what the other does, we must be careful to respond by remaining within the boundaries of our own morality. Strategic thinking is necessary, but not at the cost of our morality/humanity. We must not allow the inhumanity of the other to strip us of our humanity.

The best way to ensure that this war on terror does not escalate is by advancing a new discourse. Unlike the present discourse whose central themes are Islamic terrorism and Western colonialism, we need to explore themes that talk about bridging the gap between Islamic values and Muslim practices, and democratic values and American foreign policy. The new discourse will emerge if the moderates within the Muslim world and in the West seriously begin collective exercises in self-reflection and self-criticism to bridge the chasm between values and actions, between deeds and words, and between ideas and realities.

Chapter 8

An American Muslim Perspective of the Muslim World

Islam and Global Change

We now live in an era when change is the order of the day. In the post-cold war era, not only has change become routine, but it is also taking place in more fundamental ways than ever before. At every level – individual, societal, national, multi-national and global (systemic) – agents, structures, processes and systems are undergoing change. Both simple and fundamental forms of change are taking place. Simple forms of change include change in certain processes like diplomacy or trade. Change could also mean a power shift, from Democrats to Republicans controlling Congress, for example. Fundamental changes suggest transformation at structural and systemic levels. They indicate changes in regimes and in the nature of systems themselves. Changes from communist to capitalist economies, or authoritarian to democratic regimes are structural changes. Shifts from bipolar systems to uni-polar systems are an example of systemic change.

Individuals are becoming more cosmopolitan. While the scope and nature of their lives is becoming global they are also working towards defining their identities more sharply, often strongly grounded in something local, such as ethnicity. Identities are standing out and transforming societies into multi-cultural and multi-ethnic collectives existing under the unifying pressures of globalism and the fragmenting influence of difference. The nation state is under pressure and its future is in serious question. Even at the global systemic level, structural transformations are reorganizing the world order. In this decade itself, States like the USSR and Yugoslavia have disappeared and nearly twenty new states have emerged. While the breakup of these states suggests fragmentation, the strengthening of the EU, the impetus that NAFTA and ASEAN have gained, suggests counter forces of integration at work.

Making sense of these powerful currents of change is not easy. Most of the changes are clearly being driven by technological revolutions in transportation, communication and information industries. The process of time-space compression so strikingly illustrated by the Internet has brought the world within everyone's reach, and everyone within each other's world. Human agents armed with a global reach and unprecedented prosperity are daring to dream dreams beyond the existing political, economic and social infrastructure of the world. In the pursuit of these global dreams human agents are systematically restructuring our global institutions to facilitate globalization. But these endeavors are also resulting in unintended consequences of global dimensions, such as environmental degradation, income disparities, widespread social strife and incidences of ethnic and religious cleansing. All these trends are making our time one of the most challenging as well as fascinating periods in human history.

Besides all these changes there are two other developments that Muslims need to be particularly aware of. They are:

1. The Globalization of Islam
2. The "minoritization" of Islam

Globalization of Islam implies two things. One that Islam, by virtue of migration and conversion is found everywhere. Two that the general understanding of Islam is rising above its local manifestations and is gaining a homogenous interpretation that is widely shared by the global *Ummah*. While the first claim is self-evident the second is a bit tendentious. Critics will surely point to the differences among various Muslim groups, doctrinal as well as ritualistic, and deny any globally shared understanding of Islam besides the fundamentals of monotheism. Nevertheless, I do believe that on many issues, such as educational development, intellectual revival and opening of *ijtihad*, more and more Muslims are beginning to come closer rather than depart from each other's positions. I shall defend this claim more systematically at some other time. At this moment all I am saying is that on many issues, more and more Muslims are thinking alike.

The second global trend is the "minoritization of Islam". In a strange fashion Islam is rapidly becoming the faith of the minorities whether in the West or in India or even in the traditional Muslim World with dominant Muslim majorities. Whether in Turkey or Egypt, in Syria or Jordan, Pakistan or Bangladesh, parties and groups who are pushing the secular modernist agenda continue to remain in the majority and enjoy support as well as control over Muslim lands and Muslim futures. Islamists of every hue remain only in the minority. Thus in the absence of Islamic governance, Muslims seeking the establishment of Islamic life and institutions, in the East and in the West, continue to live as minorities.

Development: The Missing Dimension of Globalization

The contemporary discourse on globalization has marginalized interest in issues of development. While discussions on an environmentally safe strategy for development and on sustainable development still continue, advanced economies have found that they can now find enough markets and labor in newly developed and developing countries to facilitate a truly globalized economy. Development and underdevelopment are no more central to discourses dominated by Western interests. That does not mean that development is not an issue any more. It remains a central concern for the Muslim World. Except for Malaysia and Indonesia and to some extent Turkey, most of the Muslim World remains underdeveloped in economic, political as well as human sense. Even the oil rich states of the Gulf and Maghrib, which have tried to buy modernity remain synthetically modernized. If the oil wells dry up, they might suddenly find themselves in the desert.

There are clearly two reasons for this condition in the Muslim world. One, Muslims refuse to give up their traditional and cultural ways of life that prevents the "rationalization" of their society which is necessary for ushering in a Western form of modernity. Two, they have failed to envisage an alternate path to modernization. Rejection of modernity is meaningless; it merely alienates society from the momentum of history. Underdeveloped Muslim societies will remain under foreign domination and unable to defend their legitimate interests. The Muslim World will have to come to terms with modernity, not just discursively but in a material sense as well. For this they will have to advance a systematic critique of modernity, not a normative indictment, and then follow up with an alternate vision of "historical direction" for Muslims as well as humanity. Having done that they must show changes in "facts" by transforming the material and moral conditions of their existence.

The notion of "Development" presupposes many of modernity's principles and values. It accepts the idea of "progress" operationalized in economic and material terms. It also indicates a preference for secular and democratic forms of polity. Thus development has both economic as well as politico-social dimensions. The two are inseparable. Modern forms of prosperity necessarily come with a privileging of the individual over the collective, the secular over the divine, the material over the spiritual, and reason over emotion. Many of these practices are inimical to an Islamic existence. Islam would be marginalized from the social as well as the political sphere, if the Muslim World were to adopt the European path to modernity. The case of Turkey is illustrative – a Muslim Society where the government considers it "dangerous" to teach children how to read *The Qur'an*!

Some Muslim critiques of modernity have emphasized the need for implementing Islamic *Shariah* in society and caricatured the modern West as immoral and decadent. What they have utterly failed to do is show how the implementation of fossilized articulations of *Shariah* will lead to material development of the Muslim world. Thus they see the West as purely material and embark only on a moral agenda. What we need is a balance between morality and materiality. We have to recognize their mutual dependence and articulate a path for contemporary Muslim societies that will modernize as well as moralize them. Muslims need a model of "Moral Development". These things, I must warn, are easily said than done. We do not need grand thesis replete with verse after verse of the *Qur'an* to exhort Muslims to become great Muslims. The Muslim Mullahs have been doing that without any results for over two hundred years. What we need is a strong empirically oriented vision of development, easily accessible to policy making that will not remove Islam from the center stage of Muslim existence.

Re-imagining Jerusalem: One City, One Tradition

There will be no peace in the Middle East until the dispute over Jerusalem is amicably settled. Jerusalem is sacred. In three thousand years, it did not loose its centrality to Judaism and there is no possibility that it will loose its importance to Christianity or Islam.

One cannot resolve the issue of Jerusalem through promises of aid, geopolitical calculations or urban planning. Many secular analysts in the West erroneously believe that religion itself will lose its pre-eminence, making the sacredness of Jerusalem immaterial. However, one cannot deny that along with the rise and fall of communism and the emergence of liberal democracy and globalization, the global resurgence of religion and its burgeoning political influence is one of the most important developments of the twentieth century.

In Israel, religious parties have increased their share of Knesset members. In India, Hindu nationalism is ascendant. The West could not wish Iran away. Religion and its political power are here to stay. If anything, we will see an even greater role of religion in domestic and world politics.

As long as religious identities remain strong in the region and elsewhere, the status of Jerusalem will be contested and the struggle for sovereignty over Jerusalem will not diminish. Plans that are premised on material calculations of power and wealth, using threat and aid, will alone be insufficient in resolving the conflict over Jerusalem. Political solutions to religious problems usually fail. The problem is a symbolic one and will need a major symbolic component in the solution.

The solution I recommend is a collective theological initiative toward reconstruction of Jerusalem's identity. The current discourse on Jerusalem imagines it as a contested city, claimed by three different religious communities. The concept is so aptly captured in the title of Karen Armstrong's book on Jerusalem – *One city, Three Faiths.*

As long as Jerusalem is seen as one City desired by three different communities, it would remain contested. Such an imagination presupposes inevitable and eternal conflict. Jerusalem cannot be imagined as three cities desired by three faiths, as that is inconceivable. The only alternative is to imagine Jerusalem as one city desired by one faith. This re-imagination of Jerusalem eliminates conflict. Discourses constructing this particular identity of Jerusalem can and should be encouraged.

The conflict between Jews and Christians has diminished primarily because of the widespread belief that the contemporary West is a common heritage based on a Judeo-Christian ethic. However, in the last two decades, a great deal of research has acknowledged the enormous contributions that Islam has made to Western civilization. Scholars like Norman Daniels and John Esposito, and leaders like Prince Charles and President Clinton, have paid homage to Islam's civilizational contributions. Western theologians and historians now acknowledge the impact of Islam on Jewish, Christian and modern secular thought. The debt owed to Muslim philosophers and scientists is now well recorded. But unfortunately, we have not used these developments in civilizational understanding to educate Americans. Negative images of Islam continue to fester in the Western media as well as in the common Western mind.

American Muslims are taking an initiative in reconciling the three monotheistic traditions by focusing on a common Prophet – Abraham. It has generated an inter-faith dialogue that talks about the commonalities between Islam, Christianity and Judaism, and depicts them all as The Abrahamic Tradition. The Abrahamic vision imagines the three faiths as three manifestations of the same religious tradition of monotheism whose founder was Abraham. If this discourse can be fostered, widely and aggressively leading to some kind of a consensus, then Jerusalem can be imagined as one holy city of one great religious tradition. Conflict will symbolically disappear.

Muslim intellectuals in the West are seeking to replace Judeo-Christian traditions as the basis of Western civilization with the Abrahamic tradition. With a little education, some grass roots lobbying and a concerted support from the media, this idea can catch on. It benefits all and unites the three communities. Jews get to keep their

Jerusalem. Christians get an equal say in the matter, and Muslims not only get Jerusalem back but also get an irrevocably recognition from Judaism and Christianity.

But first, we all must dare to imagine ourselves as one – the followers of the Abrahamic tradition. Then Jerusalem will be ours.

Muslim Modernity in Singapore

I had the good fortune of visiting the Muslim community of Singapore in May, 2000. During my visit there, I had an intense and comprehensive interaction with the small but multi-dimensional Muslim community. My visit included over ten lectures and as many meetings with various Islamic organizations and a few institutions and think tanks established by the Singapore Government. The trip provided me a reasonably good understanding of Islam in Singapore and I wish to share it with the readers.

The first thing that struck me was that Muslims in Singapore were culturally very modernized. There were very few men who wore traditional clothes except for many of the Imams who dress like Arabs. Many women wear hijabs and dresses distinct from other women in Singapore but with a clearly modern style. My wife informs me that denim jeans and hijabs as elements of the ensemble seemed more common in Singapore than in the U.S.. Most of the Muslims in Singapore as in Malaysia are of the Malay ethnicity. We found that among hijab wearing women more women in Singapore seemed to dress in Malay style than in Western clothes. This may perhaps be explained by the relative security that Malay women feel in Malaysia where they are in majority while in Singapore Malays are a small minority (about 15%).

Singapore as a city itself is hyper-modern, with very little remnants of it past heritage. Similarly most of Singapore's mosques are also very modern with a new and wealthy look. I was very impressed with the mosques in Singapore. For years American Muslim leaders have been talking about building Islamic centers and not mosques. In a society were Muslims are in a minority, Islamic centers serve many purposes such as educational, cultural institutions as well as a place were

Muslims meet and discuss community issues. But the architecture of American mosques has yet to reflect this desire of their builders. But mosques in Singapore are very well designed community centers with pray areas, meeting rooms, conference auditoriums and even office space for a full-time staff. Unlike other places were mosques are designed only for prayer (as in Saudi Arabia for example) one feels that the architecture is asking you to leave as soon as the prayer is over. But mosques in Singapore invite, even insist, that you stay back and participate in the affairs of the community.

The second thing that is outstanding about Singaporean Muslims is their political sophistication. They are, at least their leaders are, far more politically savvy than in many parts of the Muslim World. While American Muslims are divided over trivial questions like should Muslims participate in American politics, Singaporean Muslims have nine members of parliament in an assembly that has a little over 80 members. They also have three ministers and many parliamentary secretaries who are like assistant state ministers. Singaporean Muslims have made "working with the system" an art form. Some Muslims may consider this as capitulation to a non-Muslim system. But if you look at the result, 77 well staffed and well equipped mosques in a city of just 3.8 million people, and many developmental institutions (partially supported by state funds) helping the state help Muslims and helping Muslims help themselves, you will realize that in a state which is committed to the welfare of all its people, working with the system is a wise policy.

The Muslims of Singapore have in the last three decades developed a well funded and highly organized network of institutions whose sole purpose is increasing the well being – of Singaporean Muslims within the limits of the existing political regime. Institutions like MUIS (Islamic Religious Council of Singapore), MENDAKI (Council for the Development of Singapore Muslim Community), AMP (Association of Muslim Professionals), Perdaus and the Muslim Converts Association of Singapore, have well organized programs which are working systematically to improve the educational, financial and religious conditions of Muslims in Singapore.

There are a few things that are outstanding about all these organizations. They are all modern in their character and their nature is more representative of contemporary civil society in advanced and developed nations than any traditional, medieval Islamic institution. Also unlike traditional Islamic institutions found in other parts of the Muslim world they are not uni-dimensional. That is to say that they do not just focus on the religious *talim* (education) of the individuals and ignore everything else. All these institutions, *Alhamdulillah*, are multi-dimensional. They focus on religious as well as social, cultural and material well being of the communities they are trying to serve. Somehow the Muslims of Singapore have understood the meaning of the term "falah" (well being) much better than other Muslim minorities, especially in India and the U.S..

There are several reasons why the Muslims of Singapore have succeeded in developing such self-help institutions and a healthy attitude towards community development. One, they are part of a larger community of Singaporeans who are completely dedicated to material well being and economic progress. The Muslims of Singapore combine their Islamic desire for moral well being with their Singaporean instinct for material progress and have succeeded in manifesting a balanced approach to community development. Two, the leadership in most of these organizations comes from a professional background and they are not dominated by the Muslim clergy who are often the biggest barriers to any kind of change in the Muslim World. Unlike say South Asia and the Arab World Singapore does not have many polemical and recalcitrant Mullahs going around condemning modernity and all kinds of departures from medieval practices. Even the religious leaders of Singapore, in spite of their Al-Azhar training are very balanced and realistic.

Finally the government of Singapore, its authoritarian character not withstanding, is not only accommodating of Islam and Muslim aspirations but is also willing to actively assist the Muslim community in helping itself. Often this assistance translates into either legislation that may facilitate the realization of Muslim aspirations (AMLA for example) or in financial grants that often run into millions of dollars. The government has also been very good in providing the community land for building mosques too. During the recent "madrasah affair" the government showed willingness to not only work with Muslim leaders but also seek their active participation in policy making. While the government is a bit strict when it comes to political ideologies, it is not only open but also quite benevolent on issues of welfare and development.

The biggest the most powerful and the most important Muslim institution in Singapore is MUIS (The Majlis Ugama Islam Singapura) also known as the Islamic Religious Council of Singapore. It was established as a statutory body in 1968 when the Administration of Muslim Law Act (AMLA) came into effect. Under AMLA, MUIS is to advise the President of Singapore on all matters relating to Islam in Singapore. The role of MUIS is to ensure that the many and varied interests of Singapore's Muslim community are looked after. In this regard MUIS is responsible for the promotion of religious, social, educational, economic and cultural activities in accordance with the principles and traditions of Islam as enshrined in the *Holy Qur'an* and *Sunnah.*

The self-stated principal functions of MUIS are: administration of *zakat, fitrah, wakaf,* pilgrimage affairs and *Dawah* activities. They also administer, maintain and build all the mosques in Singapore. They are in charge of the coordination of Islamic educational programs and issuance of *fatwas* (religious rulings), provision of study grants to Muslim students and provision of financial relief to poor and needy Muslims and new converts.

In many ways MUIS is like an Islamic monopoly that exclusively controls some of the most important Islamic activities in Singapore such as resource distribution and Islamic institutional development. It has close government ties, and is supported and to some extent financed by the government. Most of its resources come from within the community and so far MUIS has served it well. MUIS is Singapore's attempt to manage Islam as a public sector enterprise. Fortunately all the brothers and sisters who work for MUIS are dedicated Muslims and instead of MUIS becoming a government arm that deals with Muslims, it has become a Muslim representation to the government. Under the leadership of dedicated leaders like Haji Maarof Haji Salleh (The President) and Syed Harron Aljunied (Secretary) his selfless lieutenant, MUIS is doing great service to the Muslims of Singapore.

Perhaps the development of Singapore's Muslim institutions is also indicative of the political limits within which Muslims exist and operate. Most of the Muslims in Singapore belong to the minority community of Malays. Thus they are double in minority. They are not only a religious minority but also an ethnic minority. For those not familiar with Singapore's ethnic composition may not realize the significance of this double minority status. For example consider the community of Chinese Christians. They too are a religious minority but because they belong to the dominant ethnicity (Chinese constitute 74% of Singapore's population) they have a greater access to power then Muslims who are both Malay and Muslim. Because most Muslims are Malay (nearly 90% of 400,000) they have to suffer a degree of marginalization given the Singaporean fear that Malaysia, a Malay power from whom it broke away in 1966, may still be harboring desires of reunification.

These political limits, in combination with the material instinct of the Singaporean Muslims and the lack of genuine indigenous Islamic intellectual traditions has made Islam in Singapore modern but mundane, developed but also tamed. The Muslims and their organizations are either struggling to get their "fair share" of Singapore's prosperity or fighting to defend their ethnic and religious identity. They are far from providing moral and political leadership to Singapore. Perhaps the growth of Chinese converts to Islam may facilitate more active participation by Muslims in shaping the character of Singapore.

Talking to the majority community in Singapore, as I did at various think tanks such as the Institute of Defense Studies and Institute of Policy Studies, one realizes that it is a society without a soul and without any authentic identity. In simple terms it is what its material success makes it; a fabulous mall in the middle of a big pond. But this lack of a moral and normative core is an opportunity that Muslims of Singapore have not yet fully exploited. As perhaps the only community more dedicated to values of life than values of things, they can not only set the moral agenda of Singapore but also lead by example. But for this the Muslims of Singapore need a vision of the self and of Singapore both distinct and superior to the one advanced by the present "mood" in Singapore. For that they need an intellectually vibrant Muslim community, fearlessly participating not only in politics but also in all social and cultural aspects of Singapore. Singaporeans are too ethnically loyal. They all live in ethnic frameworks in spite of cosmetic attempts at unification such as diversified housing. Muslims of Singapore must step out of their "Malay ghetto" and occupy the universalist position still vacant. They must act not just in self interest but also in the moral and spiritual interest of Singapore so that one day it may have a soul and be grateful to Muslims for their contributions.

Bangladesh: A Poor Muslim Democracy

Bangladesh is an interesting puzzle. It is representative of the contemporary postmodern condition when nothing is clearcut. It is at once both highly developed as well as underdeveloped. Bangladesh is a country that is economically backward and politically quite advanced. Many political and social scientists have often equated democracy with development and capitalism with political freedom. Bangladesh belies both these assumptions. It is a reasonably free society while being one of the world's poorest economies. Even the Freedom House ratings, which are quite biased against non-Western societies rank Bangladesh as a reasonably free state.

For a nation that has existed for only thirty years it is quite an achievement to have had two elected women heads of state. In fact, if one were to compare the Bangladeshi democracy with the American democracy at the age of thirty, the nation of Bengalis will come out quite favorably. In 200 years, the U.S. has yet to allow a woman to run the state.

Bangladesh's two women heads of state are former Prime Minister Sheikh Hasina of Awami league and the present Prime Minister and leader of BNP, Begum Zia. It is amazing that this country of a hundred million Muslims looks like a matriarchical society, belying another myth that associates patriarchy with Muslim culture. Bangladesh apparently is destined to destroy widely held myths. First by its very origins it has exploded the myth of Islamic unity. By breaking away from Pakistan, Bangladesh has shown that *asabiyyah* (Ibn Khaldun's term for ethnic solidarity) can at times overwhelm Islamic unity. Perhaps the rupture of the united Pakistan is more a commentary on the lip service given to Islamic brotherhood by Muslim leaders than the relative powers of Islam and ethnicity. Nonetheless, the very existence of Bangladesh is a blow to the rhetoric of Islamic unity that most Muslims like to crow about. The present day Muslims of Bangladesh live in greater harmony with its 11% Hindu minority than they did with Muslims of non-Bengali origins.

Bangladesh is not the only case where interests other than Islamic unity have proven more powerful. The quick disintegration of the United Arab Republic, a union of Syria and Egypt that combined Islam, *asabiyyah* (Arab nationalism) and external threat (from Israel), is another case of Islamic entities splitting for interests other than Islam.

The second myth that Bangladesh has exposed is the claim by some Muslims and many westerners that Islam and democracy are incompatible. Bangladesh while not exactly an exemplary democracy or an advertisement for Islamic governance has nevertheless succeeded in demonstrating that a community dominated by Muslims can have Islam as the state religion and still provide democratic rights to its citizens and freedom of religion to its minorities.

Yes, there are cases of religious discrimination and harassment of minorities in Bangladesh. For example in 1992, when the Babri Masjid was destroyed in India by Hindu nationalists nearly 80 Hindu temples were desecrated in Bangladesh as an act of revenge. If what the Hindus did was a travesty, then what the Bangladeshi Muslims did was much worse. Also in April, unknown miscreants blew a Roman Catholic Church. But these infrequent tragedies apart, Bangladesh is striving to be a good state that treats all its citizens justly.

Its constitution at least is determined to do justice to all. It recognizes the primacy of Islam (Article 2A) but guarantees the freedom of religion of all communities (Article 41). Article 11 of the constitution asserts that the Republic will be a democracy that respects all the human rights and freedoms of all its citizens. Article 39 specifically protects the freedom of speech and expression of every citizen (39a) and 39b guarantees the freedom of the press.

Cynics, especially those who neither understand, nor respect democratic principles, maybe tempted to underestimate the importance of their constitution. However, the key is in its implementation. In the era of globalization and global interdependence, having these rights enshrined in the constitution is an important first step. International pressure, especially from NGOs and human rights activists has a greater impact on states that already claim to respect these rights. Often moving court in cases of human rights violations provides effective remedy. But in states whose constitutions do not already enshrine human rights; states can continue to violate their own citizens with impunity leaving no recourse to domestic as well as international human rights activists.

Bangladeshis have also shown that Muslim societies allow women more opportunities for self-expression in the public arena than they are given credit for. Bangladeshi women are not only well integrated into the political arena but are also quite active in the economic sphere. The micro-enterprise project (Grameen Bank) initiated by Dr. Muhammad Yunus has shown that empowering women is an important strategy to fight poverty and underdevelopment. Bangladeshi women have shown that while remaining within the moral sphere of Islamic values, women can play an important role in the economic well being of their immediate families and the political well being of their nation.

Bangladesh is a highly developed state in political terms. But sadly it exposes an American myth that prosperity follows freedom. Bangladesh is a "poor democracy". Its per capita income is less than $500 a year. 36% of the population is below poverty level and nearly 35% of the population is unemployed. Annually a large section of the country is submerged in floods and as sea levels rise with global warming Bangladesh will face more drastic environmental threats with devastating economic implications.

Lack of industrialization, poor infrastructures, and untapped human resources will continue to challenge Bangladesh in its quest for economic well being. Poverty and disasters will continue to test the moral and political fiber of the nation. There are no shortcuts out of the environmental and economic troubles of Bangladesh. But we must remember that in spite of all its difficulties, Bangladeshis have found a way to live in freedom, respect each other's dignity and remain connected with God.

Khatami and Prospects for Reform in Iran

The last Iranian election has given the pro-reform incumbent President Khatami and his supporters a resounding victory. Khatami won 77% of the vote against nine conservative challengers. In 1997, he had won 69% of the vote. Khatami's huge victory is a clear mandate for reform. Both the conservative clerics aligned with the *Vilayat-e-Faqih* (religious head of state) Ali Khameini and the reformist positioned the present election as a referendum on Khatami's reformist agenda. The results are loud and clear.

Since his election in 1997 Khatami has been struggling to alter the politics of Iran. Iran's governmental structure has a division of power between three institutions; The President, *The Majlis* (parliament) and the *Vilayat-e-Faqih*. The president and the members of the Parliament are elected and act essentially as the legislature and executive. The religious head is the head of the judiciary and the guardian of the Islamic constitution of the country. While all three institutions are important, the religious head has the power to override the Parliament as well as the President. In this peculiar arrangement the un-elected office of the religious head has more power than the elected offices.

The underlying theory behind this idea is that Islamic law is given (not open to any interpretation) and the *Fuqaha* (Islamic clerics) are the sole knowers of what this law is. The ideological objective of an Islamic state according to the Iranian arrangement is above all else to implement Islamic law. This arrangement also assumes that the *Fuqaha* are just, incorruptible and of unimpeachable moral character (this is an assumption there is neither empirical nor Qur'anic evidence to support this claim) and therefore can impose their understanding of Islam on the President and the Parliament.

Over the years, the clergy in Iran have proven that they are neither just nor incorruptible and have consequently lost people's confidence. They have used the security apparatus of the state, which is not controlled by the President, to harass anyone who has dared to raise their voice against the tyranny of the clergy. Over the years many journalists and thinkers have been jailed and abused by the clergy controlled security services.

Over the years Iran has been suffering economically and its population has been growing astronomically. Iran has doubled its population from 30 to 60 million since 1979. International sanctions have also hurt Iran's economy. As things got worse and people became increasingly disenchanted with the powers that be, the conservative clergy resorted to stricter and stricter imposition of the symbolic elements of Islam such as the veiling of women. They have also attacked institutions of the free media to curtail criticism. Iranians not only felt disenchanted with the government and its rhetoric but also felt stifled by its heavy-handed policies.

It was in such an environment that Muhammad Khatami came as a breath of fresh air promising to develop a civil society in Iran. He promised his people three things: more freedom, more representation and the obedience of law by citizens as well as the government. The conservatives, needless to say, oppose all the three items on Khatami's agenda. More freedom marginalizes them from society by reducing the spheres where they can exercise power and control. More representation means more and more lay people coming to power and diluting the domination of the power hungry clergy. And finally forcing the government to obey laws essentially undermines the current status of the clergy as above the law. They enforce Islamic law but do not apply the law to themselves. Khatami's promise to make government accountable to the people and law abiding has not been welcomed by the clergy.

So far the struggle in Iran has been between those who advocate reform in the system and the conservative clergy who resist it. The tidal wave of support for Khatami and reform must have surely shaken the conservatives. It is clear that the people of Iran are tired of the dictatorial tendency of the conservative *ulema* and it is time they backed off to let the moderate and more considerate scholars like Khatami fulfill the destiny of Iran.

The near future of Iran will be tumultuous and challenging. The reformist strengthened as never before will push hard for change. The conservatives threatened as never before will probably dig in and will not budge without a fight. I am hopeful that wisdom will prevail and the conservatives will not resort to violence and force to resist reform. An overwhelming majority of Iranians, especially the youth, want change. Too much resistance could lead to a revolution or worse an Algeria like impasse.

Muhammad Khatami is the kind of leader that Al-Farabi and Plato use to dream about — a Philosopher King. Khatami is a cleric who has excelled in Islamic scholarship. At the international level Khatami has led the global call for a civilizational dialogue. Americans would be surprised to know that Khatami has translated parts of Tocqueville's *Democracy in America* into Persian. He along with the philosopher Abdul Kareem Soroush is the voice of justice, moderation and balance in a society deeply influenced by faith and ideology. In the last few years, Khatami along with Soroush has advocated reform that would give the people more power and increase the democratic content of Iranian polity.

Iran's transition from a totalitarian state under Khomeini to a moderate and more liberal democracy under Khatami is a priceless laboratory for the entire Muslim World that is struggling to escape authoritarianism. Iran's experience is invaluable in assisting Muslim thinkers in their quest for an Islamic democracy. It is hopeful that in the coming months all the people of Iran conduct themselves with patience and wisdom and give the rest of the *Ummah* more to look up to. This election of Iran was not only a victory for those who want reform in Iran, but also a victory for those who want reform in the entire Muslim World. Iran is proving that not only democracy but also an Islamic democracy is viable in the contemporary Muslim world.

Lingering Questions Over the Tragedy of Afghanistan

If a man kills a believer intentionally, his recompense is Hell, to abide therein (forever): And the wrath and the curse of Allah are upon him, and a dreadful penalty is prepared for him. – Qur'an 4: 93

The recent history of Afghanistan is sad and troubling. The misery and suffering of the people is there for all to see. There is no doubt that they have had to pay a very high price for their freedom and political independence. As a distant and far removed ethnic brethren of the Afghan people, my heart aches for them. But as a Muslim, engaged in the *Jihad* (for me personally *Ijtihad* is not only the highest but also the best form of *Jihad*), for the revival of Islamic civilization, the happenings in Afghanistan are deeply disturbing.

From 1978 to 1988 the people of Afghanistan fought against the Soviet Union, a communist super power, to free their nation and their people from political and ideological domination. In 1988 the Soviet Union withdrew its forces, but it was only in 1992 that the brave Mujahideen finally made a triumphant entrance into Kabul, to once and for all, bury communism and hoist the flag of Islam.

Most of the Muslim world admired and loved these brave fighters, who were not only fighting for their land but also for the religion of Allah. I remember as a teenager, going from house to house collecting goatskins after sacrifice on Eid and sending them to Islamic organizations supporting the Afghan Mujahideen. Years later, I remember I was still praying for their victory and praising them in my *Qutbas*.

Then, something happened. They marched into Kabul and I prayed that Allah would see this act as similar to Prophet Muhammad's (pbuh) triumphant and historic march into Makkah. But there ends the honeymoon and the romance in the minds of admiring Muslims. To our horror these Mujahideen turned upon each other. To kill, slaughter and maim. The ferocity with which they had attacked the Soviets was once again unleashed upon each other.

It does not matter who is to blame for the Afghan tragedy. What mattered was that for the sake of power these soldiers of Allah, killed other soldiers of Allah. When the Soviets killed Afghans, we called them the enemies of Allah and Islam. What do we call the Afghans who killed Muslims and Afghans? Mujahideen? What was more devastating was the question; if these people who we thought were fighting for Islam could so brutally kill their own people for power, then what was the true motivation for their war against the Soviet Union?

From 1992 to 1996, Afghanistan under the control of Mujahideen was engulfed in a bloody civil war, which did not spare even women and children. Was this the new face of political Islam?

Then I started studying the phenomenon and realized that it was not just their faith and their courage that had led to the victory against the Soviet Union. The U.S. had spent over $14 Billion in military aid, some of which was misappropriated by Pakistani bureaucrats, but most of which actually funded the Afghan war.

The more I studied, the more I learnt about the role of the Pakistani army and the CIA in defeating the Soviets. The victory of the Mujahideen, who after the war turned upon Muslims with the same murderous vengeance that they had used against the communists, seemed less and less miraculous. I also learnt that it was the stinger missiles given by the U.S. and not necessarily the spirit of these Mujahideen that had eliminated the air advantage held by the Soviet forces.

In 1994, a new force, once again using the name of Islam appeared almost out of nowhere – the Taliban. Afghan kids who were refugees in Pakistan suddenly came out of their schools armed with assault rifles, trucks, tanks and anti-tank rockets and bazookas. Indeed it is a tragedy that as schools languish from lack of adequate resources, Afghanistan is full of hidden stocks of weaponry, adequate to fight a modern war.

These new soldiers of Islam, with weapons obtained from mysterious sources, took less than two years to defeat the mighty Mujahideen, the conquerors of a super power, and captured Kabul in 1996. By now I had become cynical about the Mujahideen. Without the support of the U.S. funds, CIA training, intelligence and satellite information, and the supervision of the Pakistani army, the great Mujahideen with a decade of war experience were no match for the new kids straight out of school.

Apparently the sources of strength for the Mujahideen had now become the sources of strength for the Taliban. Pakistan needed a stable Afghanistan. The U.S. needed to calm the region and prevent the spread of Islamic rebellion into Central Asia where it was seeking to replace Russian hegemony. And the Saudis saw the possibility for another Wahhabi state, especially on the other side of Iran, to sandwich the Shia regime in Tehran.

Whatever the interests of other nations, the Taliban somehow found the resources to defeat the Mujahideen, whom they called the enemies of Islam. And until now, we thought that the Mujahideen were among those inspired by the spirit of the Sahaba.

Since 1996, the Taliban, and the Mujahideen now in alliance with the communists, continued to kill each other, Muslims, fellow brethren, in the name of Islam.

Salafi scholars endorsed the Taliban regime as Islamic and guided by the *Shariah* (Islamic law). These are the same scholars who had once praised the spirit of the *Sahaba* in the *Mujahideen*. Young Muslims rushed to defend the Taliban or even join them. But how could Muslims quickly forget that the Taliban were dedicated to killing their former Islamic heroes. Sure we all know that some of the former Mujahideen, including the Bin Laden brigade had joined the Taliban. But still the famous, now dead hero, Masood Shah was opposed to the Taliban.

In 2001 the Taliban, by supporting Bin Laden accused of perpetrating the horrible attacks on America on September 11, implicated themselves and invited the wrath of the U.S. It was really tragic and even pathetic to watch as these great soldiers of Allah got wiped out by the U.S. and the Northern Alliance (composed of former Mujahideen and the communists). Not only were the Taliban defeated comprehensively, they also showed a lot of cowardice by surrendering and running, belying their own claims that they would either defeat the U.S. or die in the process. Many Muslim experts agreed with them calling Afghanistan the "graveyard of empires". All of them were proven wrong as the U.S. accomplished most of their goals of eliminating the Taliban and establishing a pro-western and pro-democracy government.

Muslims take great pride in the military achievements of past Muslims especially when they are against ostensibly more powerful players; for example the success of the Afghan Mujahideen against the Soviets. Moreover, we tend to attribute success not to material conditions such as strategy, arsenal, technology, etc. but to the "Iman" of the fighters. The Mujahideen won because they were great Muslims (in this narration the critical and sustained support from U.S. and Pakistan is ignored or rarely mentioned). But then how do we explain the defeat of the Taliban? Were they bad Muslims? Had they lost Allah's favor and were defeated and humiliated in the eyes of the world?

Is there a lesson here? I see only questions. What does it mean to fight for Islam? Does it mean to kill in the name of Islam or to live by Islamic values? How can Islamic values be realized in societies without the establishment of peace? Is not the word Islam a conjugation of the word Salam --peace? Do not Muslims wish peace to each other, upon the Prophets and those who served Islam?

One of God's 99 names is Peace, none include *harb*, or war. Is war the only way to serve Islam? What do we make of those who supposedly fight for Islam then turn around and kill Muslims? Did not the Prophet say that under no circumstance shall a Muslim kill another Muslim? Isn't the blood of a Muslim forbidden to another Muslim? Did not the Prophet also say that an ordinary Muslim is more important than even the Kabba? How then can we take the killing of Muslims by other Muslims so lightly? Why do our great *Ulema* not speak out against this? What happened to the *fatwa* industry? Why isn't there a *fatwa* banning the killings of Muslims in the name of *jihad*?

What fundamental differences existed between the Mujahideen and the Taliban or among the Mujahideen themselves that allowed these servants of Islam to violate this very fundamental principle of

Islam — not to kill another Muslim. Allah may forgive them for what they did. But will Allah forgive those of us who thought of them as heroes of Islam?

> *Never should a believer kill a believer; but (if it so happens) by mistake, (compensation is due): If one (so) kills a believer, it is ordained that he should free a believing slave, and pay compensation to the deceased's family, unless they remit it freely. If the deceased belonged to a people at war with you, and he was a believer, the freeing of a believing slave (is enough). If he belonged to a people with whom ye have treaty of Mutual alliance, compensation should be paid to his family, and a believing slave be freed. For those who find this beyond their means, (is prescribed) a fast for two months running: by way of repentance to God: for God hath all knowledge and all wisdom. — Qur'an 4: 92*

Allah says in the above ayah: "If the deceased belonged to a people at war with you, and he was a believer, the freeing of a believing slave (is enough)." When are the Taliban and the Mujahideen going to release thousands of believing slaves in lieu of the thousands of believers they have killed? If the Taliban believe in the *Shariah*, surely they are aware of this ayah. When are they going to impose the *Shariah* on themselves? When do they plan to start living by the injunctions of the *Qur'an* and stop killing other Muslims?

It is not guns but ideas that will revive Islamic civilization. It is not killing but thinking that will establish divine governance. It is not in death but in life that Islam is manifest. We worship Peace (*Al Salam*) not war. Remember we are the only people who actually worship peace.

Five Reasons Why Hindu Nationalism Will Fail

The rise of Hindu Nationalism and the growing political clout of the Sangh Parivar is manifesting in systematic violation of the human rights of Muslim and Christian minorities not to mention sustained violence against them, their properties and their institutions. Nevertheless, I am confident that this wave of religious nationalism in India will eventually subside and the country will return to its default state of generally harmonious condition. I am convinced that Hindu nationalism is a parochial movement that serves parochial interests. If the BJP remains in power at the national level long enough, its narrow interests will be exposed and it will be reduced to the size it merits (as in 1986).

Inside/Outside: A Tradition of Dual Discrimination:

Identity movements whether in the interest of ethnicity, class or a nation-state seek to strengthen identity by forging solidarity inside and celebrating difference outside. Most successful nationalist movements have forged a national identity and then used that identity to rapidly move the nation along the path of modernization. Sometimes it took wars with neighbors and imperial campaigns abroad to both forge a strong national identity and to rapidly modernize. Those nations that sought to create difference, both inside and outside, have failed. The German state while distinguishing itself from other nation states also chose to create an internal difference between Germans and Jews leading to the holocaust and a massive defeat of that state.

The Hindutva movement in its search for modernization and a national identity is also seeking to create differences inside and out- side. While on the outside it celebrates "Indianness" in the inside it celebrates "Hindu parochialism" that excludes Muslims, Christians and millions of lower class Hindus. So far its nationalist jingoism has not led India into a major war, but its misplaced religious nationalism has already created deep schisms within the nation itself. In seeking to forge a strong Hindu identity, it has merely succeeded in planting deep divisions within the society. Such intensity which is generated more thorough hatred of an "internal other" (The Muslim, the Christian and the Dalit) will eventually lead to the implosion of the movement itself.

No Domestic Vision

Hindu nationalist in spite of their strong fervor and their insis- tence that India and Hinduism are synonymous, have really failed to provide Indians with a vision of India. What will happen to India if all Indians accepted their so-called Hindu roots? What does "Ram Rajya" mean? How can we recognize that Ram Rajya is in place? Through justice and security for the minorities? Through safety and guaranteed development and growth for the down trodden? Who knows what it means. Does Ram Rajya mean demolishing mosques and replacing them with temples? I do not wish to belabor it, the point is simple, what kind of India does the Hindutva movement envisage?

Powerful, nuclear, rich and with enormous respect internationally, including of course the veto power in the Security Council. But let me remind the readers that this is not a vision, this is a wish list very similar to the dreams of Brazil Grande. Every Third World post-colonial country from Egypt to Indonesia has entertained these dreams. The phenomenon is basically one where the slave imagines herself as the master.

The Hindutva movement dreams of an India that enjoys its "due respect" in global affairs. I believe this dream will un-do Hindu nationalism. No movement can be successful without identifying parameters of internal development and establishing moral standards to which it will adhere. What are the moral standards that Hindu nationalism wishes to be measured by? Democratic credentials? Respect for human rights, for social justice or for tolerance. None of the above. Hindu nationalism is a naked will to power, brutal, amoral and purposeless. Until it can find moral direction within itself and clearly articulate the indicative virtues of Ram Rajya, it is bound to fail.

India's Complex Diversity

India, culturally speaking, is a very well endowed state. India's diversity is very complex and multilayered. India is multilingual, multireligious and multi-ethnic and multi-racial. Within every religious community there is ethnic as well as linguistic diversity. Even within such a small sub-group as "Indian-Urdu-speaking-Shii-Muslims-of-Iranian-extraction" there is a difference in dialect between those who live in Lucknow and those who live in Hyderabad. What is even more amazing and amusing is that each community enjoys mimicking the other's Urdu accent and dialect.

In a society such as India's where diversity is celebrated with such reckless abandonment attempts to enforce a singular identity to drive any nationalist agenda is ridiculous. So far, the Vishwa Hindu Parishad (VHP) brigade has succeeded in whipping a frenzy of hatred against Muslims and other minorities. This hatred alone is acting as glue for their nationalist dreams.

Diverse and multicultural, pluralist democracies can only survive by focusing the attention of the populace on limited public goods. In the U.S., which is also a diverse democracy, freedom, security and welfare usually serve as nation building public goods. Goods that are equally valued across identities. Hindu nationalism has failed to provide any such universally valued public good that will appeal across identities. So far their "rath" is marching on the fuel of hatred for minorities.

Economic Mercantilism in the age of Globalization

Nuclear weapons, Pakistan, and Muslims may continue to act as lightening rods in the current political environment but in the long run, the enduring issue in India remains poverty and underdevelopment. A large percentage of the World's poorest people live in India. As far as India is concerned the most enduring issue for years will be the economy. The Hindutva movement's nationalist sentiments also impinge upon its economic thinking. "Swadeshi" tendencies have continued to undermine foreign direct investment, liberalization and economic globalization.

At a time when markets, industries and finance is globalizing at a breakneck speed, countries and corporations that enjoy an edge in any field are making it big. There is no doubt that India has successfully developed a cutting edge in the soft side of information technology. But in spite of having the world's largest and most sophisticated pool of infotech experts and practitioners, it has not really capitalized its advantage. Indians are enjoying the benefits of this advantage by way of cornering millions of jobs and have also had some success at the start-up games in silicon Valley.

But India as a country has not really benefited in terms of gaining technological edge over the U.S., Europe and Japan, nor has it attracted any significantly disproportionate share of FDI (foreign direct investment). Investors still view India as a Third World market rather than an economic/tech-tiger. The RSS (Rashtriya Swayamsevak Sangh) and BJP's (Bharatiya Janata Party) anti-MNC actions and attitudes have not really encouraged foreign trade or investment. They have made India an exporter of experts rather than goods and products. India is now the biggest exporter of tech-labor. Once again the blame for this must fall on the Hindutva movement's flawed and nineteenth century-type economic nationalism

Inherent Religious Pluralism in Hinduism

Hinduism is a remarkably open and diverse faith. There are no doctrinal elements in Hinduism that critically define a Hindu and a non-Hindu. It is also a religion that has over the years accommodated thousands of gods and goddesses. The opportunity to add new gods to the faith has made it inherently diverse and structurally pluralist. The Hindutva movement has tried to make Hinduism a monotheistic faith by emphasizing Ram over all other gods, but so far, it is not making much headway in these theological endeavors. Other gods and even Man-gods like Sai Baba continue to thrive and attract new devotees. This structural pluralism of the Hindu faith presents the biggest challenge to the success of Hindu nationalism.

Hinduism and its tolerance for different gods, different values and different forms of worship make it difficult to be intolerant of other faiths. Hindutva leaders have succeeded in whipping up anti-Muslim and anti-Christian sentiments by channeling political resentment against Pakistan and colonialism. While there seems to be little hope for peace with Pakistan in the immediate future, trends in global economy and costs of the low-intensity conflict will eventually force the two nations to compromise and end hostilities. Such an eventuality will diffuse the sources of anti-Muslim resentment in Hindus and also marginalize Hindutva.

The inability of Hindutva protagonists to provide an intellectual and visionary content to their ideological sentiments, will eventual expose the negativities upon which the movement is based and hasten its demise. No good has ever come out of hate. The cosmic order is not going to change in order to accommodate Hindu nationalism – a mass expression of bigotry and prejudice.

Addressing the Plight of Indian Muslims

The socio-political and economic condition of Muslims in India needs little elaboration to their ethnic brethren in the U.S. The widespread poverty and illiteracy, the sub-human living conditions, the social and cultural marginalization and political subordination is all too familiar to those of us, who care, and who have tried to remain in touch with our roots. While there are many reasons for the tragic plight of Muslims in India, often as many as there are analysts, there have been very few systematic efforts to redress the situation. More importantly, there is a marked absence of social movements that would specifically arrest the continuing decline of the living conditions of Muslims in India. Muslim energies so far have either attempted to combat the threat to Muslim identity and their religio-cultural heritage, or indulged in futile pursuits for unrealistic political goals. The responsibility for irresponsible use of the meager resources and vast energies of the community definitely lies with a remarkably ineffective leadership. An examination of the achievements of Muslim leaders in the post independence era leaves us with an inescapable conclusion that they have failed miserably.

The failure is manifest in the prevalent hostile atmosphere, the continuing economic and political marginalization of the community and the declining currency of its culture and heritage. While the historical reasons for such a present may be edifying and of significant academic interests, they are not germane to the discussion at hand. What will suffice is an articulation of the present conditions of Muslims in India in order to emphasize the need to respond in a systematic and cohesive fashion. Needless to say, the concern and willingness to help and improve their condition, on the part of the readers is assumed. Therefore this argument will not even attempt to proselytize, it will however definitely refer to the urgency, with which we need to respond.

The plight of the Muslims can be seen in two ways. The economic decline and underdevelopment can be attributed to the absence of any significant share in political power which would have enabled the community to use the state's resources to not only improve its living conditions but also to alter the structural conditions in its favor. Or, the lack of significant political power can be explained in terms of declining economic clout. While the close association between economic power and political power is self evident, what comes first is like the chicken and egg story. A possible route to take is, to make the intervention on the economic front. Any moves to participate in the political battles at home will be seen as unwelcome and hostile by an already angry and belligerent majority. Intervention on the religious front will not only invite the same reaction from the majority but also an angry response from the Muslim clergy, which might easily delegitimize our well-intentioned efforts. Thus the only way to go would be through a program for economic and social development that consciously eschews religious or political debates. Economic change will certainly have religio-political consequences. So be it. These consequences will be generated from within and not seen as injected from without, thereby allowing us to continue working towards the economic development of our brethren.

There is another way to approach the problem. I contend that the condition of Muslims in India has progressively eroded primarily due to an absence of systematic and cohesive efforts to redress the situation. The key ideas here are "systematic" and "cohesive". Without delving into any details I would like to point out that Muslim responses so far have been "reactions" to political or religious stimuli. In the absence of any forum in India that acts as the "self-conscious guardian" of Muslim interests, there is a great confusion about the state of Muslims in India. There is no clear and conscious diagnosis of the community's ills and therefore no cohesive strategy emerges for amelioration of its condition. In other words, what the Muslim community lacks is a vanguard, an intellectual community that will understand the needs of the community, articulate its goals and strategies and implement them; an intellectual body that can cement the Muslims into a cohesive and effective civil community.

Today Muslims in India are a community by virtue of a religious identity. They are not a community in any other sense. They are neither economically unified, nor politically organized sufficiently to act in unison. Even spatially they are wide spread. Thus all other (other than religion) conditions that contribute to community building, economics, politics and territoriality, are absent in Muslims in India. I once again attribute this disarray to an absence of an intellectual elite that can hold a community together. In order to do anything salutary for the Muslims in India, efforts should be directed towards the development of an "intellectual core" which can provide the much-needed direction and effectiveness and also the forum for discussion of the communities present and future. Solutions cannot be imported or planted. The West's failed efforts to modernize the Third World stand testimony to this truism. Solutions can only emerge from those who understand their own conditions of existence and are aware of their aspirations. In order to reach this mature stage a community needs to build an intellectual leadership, and not be left to the mercy of self-regarding and characterless political entrepreneurs.

How can an intellectual leadership emerge amongst the Muslims in India? This is the central question that I beg you to address. My answer is through pooling resources from all across the globe. And to do this we need to have a think tank, a center for policy development that will train and educate potential talent back home. Some effective measures and planning must be done and soon. I fear that a rather unpleasant scenario is developing in India. It is possible that we may see the emergence of a Third World within India itself. While the majority community benefits and contributes to the economic blossoming of India the Muslims may lag behind and experience a rapid degree of underdevelopment. India is growing in its private industrial sector and its information and banking related service sectors. This are the two areas in which Muslims are traditionally behind. Unless cohesive strategies are developed and mass educational efforts made the Muslims may miss the boom.

Who are the Indian Muslims?

In the fall 2000 I gave a lecture on the rise of Hindu Nationalism at the Islamic center of Minneapolis. This lecture was organized as a fundraiser to assist IMRC (Indian Muslim Relief Committee) in its efforts to raise money for various projects in India. During this lecture I asked the audience what we meant when we say that we are Indian Muslims? In the discussion after my lecture one prominent Indian Muslim leader responded, rather sanctimoniously, by quoting the *Qur'an* and describing a believer as one who believes in God, the day of judgment, His books, His prophets and his angels. And this person added that this was the definition of an Indian Muslim.

As I listened to him, I wondered how an Indian or a Hindu person would respond to this. I thought that since in this person's definition of an Indian Muslim there was no reference to India then perhaps the Hindu nationalists are correct in excluding Muslims and Islam from their definition of India. If Indian Muslims will not include India in their self-definition why should India include them in its self-definition? I sincerely believe that the sanctimonious response from the IMRC gentleman is not representative of how most Indian Muslims feel, especially those who actually live in India. In my mind there are no Indian Muslims without India.

Many Islamic activists often try to undermine the role of ethnicity while discussing the identities of Muslims. They pretend that all that matters is Islamic beliefs and the rest is insignificant. Unfortunately this is far from true. The division of Pakistan into Bangladesh and Pakistan is proof that ethnicity can sometimes be as powerful if not more powerful than religious solidarity. Even when the first Khalifah was being elected after the death of Prophet Muhammad (sas), the ethnicity/tribal identity of Abu Bakr (rah), helped him in prevailing over other candidates. Everyone present, including Umar bin Khattab (rah) agreed that it was important that the Caliph be a Quraishi, or else the entire Arabia would not obey him. Even here tribalism played a major role. Perhaps it was this episode that prompted Al Mawardi to write in his *Ahkam-e-Sultaniyyah* that a Caliph must always belong to the tribe of the Quraish. Many schools of Islamic jurisprudence and also scholars and many Muslim thinkers including Ibn Khaldun defer to Al Mawardi's thesis of the Khalifah as the Islamic theory of the Khalifah, which attaches so much significance to tribal identity.

So ethnicity is important. So how do Indian Muslims, Islamic rhetoric aside, really think of themselves? One way of describing Indian Muslims would be as Urdu speaking, but this would exclude millions of south Indian Muslims particularly from Tamil Nadu, Kerala and Karnataka. I have no exact answer to this question. When I think of myself, I know that I am a Muslim, perhaps even a good Muslim, but I also know that all that is good in me is not limited to my Muslim experience, it is also indebted to my Indianness.

Today with the rise of Hindutva, Hindu nationalism that equates Indian citizenship and culture with Hindu faith, India is experiencing an identity crisis. There is a clash of visions between the Nehruvian India, secular and multicultural and Hindutva's India where Indian means Hindu. The former includes Muslims within the concept of Indian citizenship and the latter excludes it. Indeed in many respects the Hindutva India is constructed as self that is contrasted with the Muslim other (Pakistan). According to the Hindutvawadis, if Pakistan is for Muslims then Bharat must be for Hindus, therefore there is no room for Muslims in Bharat.

In many ways, India's identity crisis is an intramural affair between secular and bigoted Hindus. Other communities have taken sides based on pragmatic and political necessities. Muslims too have aligned with communists and lower caste Hindus to stem the tide of Hindu nationalism. This is a pragmatic but a short-term solution. In the long run, Muslims must find a conceptual and integral position in the concept of India itself. For Muslims to survive in India, an inclusive and not exclusive conception of India must emerge and prevail.

It is time that Indian Muslims began a collective process of soul searching to understand who they really are and how their Indianness must be recognized and reconciled with their Muslim identity. Dreaming of Pakistan or the Holy Land of Saudi Arabia is going to neither enhance their Islamic virtue nor their status in India. Having met Pakistanis and visited Saudi Arabia I can testify that Hindus in India by and large are more respectful of Indian Muslims than many of their coreligionists. Some Pakistanis nurture a subtle prejudice that Indian Muslims have been Hinduized already and this shows immediately in unguarded conversations. Furthermore their foreign policy has done its best to make the lives of Indian Muslims as miserable as possible. The Saudis also do not treat Indian Muslims (and many others) as their equals.

It is time Indian Muslims recognized that like it or not they are Indian Muslims and they must not forget their prefix for it is not going away. Politically it is important that Indian Muslims play a more serious role in advancing a conception of India, not Nehruvian, not Hindutva, but a Muslim vision of India and within that whole they identify the place they wish to occupy. The first step towards this begins with *garv se kaho hum (Al) hindi hai.*

Kashmir: India's Challenge and Opportunity

India is on the verge of greatness. Its economy has become more and more global — and is ready to take off. It is now a technological tiger in its own right. Its mostly uninterrupted democracy since independence in 1947 is being recognized and respected globally. But the Kashmir issue is holding it back. It undermines India's global vision and its status too.

How can one aspire for international leadership when one is not a leader in one's own backyard? For India to become a great power it needs the recognition and support of crucial states in its region — and Pakistan is one of them. If Pakistan were to become an ally of India, not only would India be more secure vis-à-vis China, but it would also find it easier to realize its goal to become a permanent member of the UN Security Council. India would have greater international influence, which always translates into economic and material benefits.

All of these considerations underscore why a peaceful resolution of the Kashmir dispute is so vital for India. But such a turn of events would not only make India an important global power; South Asia, including Pakistan, would become more secure in the process. And the resulting lower defense budgets would mean more trade and more prosperity for the region as a whole.

But the Kashmir dispute has persisted in a rather intractable fashion for over fifty-four years now. It has stunted growth in the region and limited the scope of Indian influence. It all goes back to the days of independence and Hari Singh, the Hindu Maharaja of the predominantly Muslim state Kashmir. In 1947, Hari Singh saw himself forced to join the Indian union in order to secure his power. Prime Minister Jawaharlal Nehru — whose family ancestors hailed from Kashmir — was only too willing to help out. India sent airborne troops to aid the Maharaja against Pakistani-supported insurgents.

Since that time, both Pakistan and the Muslims of Kashmir have viewed the partition as unfair. It did not help matters that Nehru retracted on earlier promises for a plebiscite. The dispute over Kashmir festered for decades and then erupted when Kashmiris — clearly with the help of Pakistan — launched a military insurgency against India in 1986. Since then, India has used its military to fight the uprising and keep Kashmir within its fold, often committing brutal human rights violations against Kashmiri Muslims.

But with the growth of the Mujahideen phenomenon and the emergence of the Arab-Afghans, Kashmiris have benefited from the support of Muslim fighters hailing from Pakistan, Afghanistan and the Arab world. India has responded by accusing Pakistan of facilitating a campaign of terror against India. In the last ten years, the two nations have engaged in several low-intensity conflicts. The struggle between India's military in Kashmir and Kashmiri militants (and their international allies) has also continued as a corollary war between the two regional nuclear powers.

India must find a diplomatic route out of this military hole that it is digging for itself. After all, even the biggest on India's side realize that Pakistan will prefer to escalate, even use nuclear weapons, rather than surrender to India. For this reason, war is not a real option. Plus, even a war that does not escalate and remains a limited conventional war is still bad for India. India's present economy would be badly hurt and its high-tech leap potential stunted if the country had to sustain large-scale military operations indefinitely.

It must also realize that it cannot walk the path towards greatness by trampling on the legitimate aspirations of its own people. It will have to address the concerns of Kashmiris more honestly. Ultimately, India stands to gain more by resolving the Kashmir issue than by keeping it on the boil. The day the nuclear threshold was reached in South Asia, that day all military solutions to the Kashmiri issue evaporated. The gateway to greater international influence for India is through Kashmir. The sooner New Delhi realizes this, the quicker it will get there.

One of the byproducts of the American war on terrorism is the growing recognition in Washington that outstanding conflicts such as the dispute in Kashmir and the Arab-Israeli struggle cannot be allowed to fester indefinitely. Increasingly disparate voices in the administration as well as in the Congress have expressed their acknowledgement that the tragic events of Sept. 11th and its aftermath has opened a window of opportunity to bring peace to these beleaguered regions.

While there are those who believe that terrorism is essentially a security matter and should therefore be handled militarily, there are saner voices that argue that sources of terrorism are vastly complex and while immediate threats from groups like Al-Qaeda must be dealt with militarily, promotion of justice, peace, democracy and development is the only way to minimize terrorism in the long term.

Having said that, I must point out that the Kashmir dispute is not an easy mess to unravel. Ethnicity, religion, nationalism, state repression, systematic human rights violations and terrorism are all important ingredients of this hot South Asia curry. In many ways it is similar to the Arab-Israeli conflict but its military implications are more sinister since the primary adversaries in the Kashmir dispute – India and Pakistan – are both nuclear powers.

In both these conflicts the role of religion, Muslim-Jewish tensions in the Middle East and the Hindu-Muslim rivalry in South Asia, add complexity to a geopolitical struggle. The presence of occupied peoples in both areas further heightens the humanitarian tragedy of the conflict. The historical memories of three wars in each region have developed entrenched sentiments of hatred that make rational compromises very difficult to pursue. While Kashmir is not as vital to Hindu and Muslim faiths as Jerusalem is to Jews and Muslims, nonetheless the involvement of religion exacerbates the conflict and makes resolution very difficult. There are at least four significant issues that make resolving the Kashmir dispute a more difficult challenge than Palestine.

U.S. role in peace making: First of all unlike in the Middle East where all parties involved recognize the centrality of the U.S. to any peaceful outcome, India is opposed to any third party involvement in the Kashmir dispute. While Pakistan and the Kashmiri liberation movements have actively sought to internationalize the dispute to invite third party arbitration either from the Muslim World, the U.S. or from the UN, India has steadfastly maintained that the dispute is a bilateral issue between India and Pakistan and a solution must therefore come without intervention from outside the region. The ability of any U.S. initiative to find a resolution to the problem depends on the willingness of all parties to recognize it as either an agency for arbitration or a facilitator of peace negotiations. Basically it hinges on the question; will India accept a new and larger involvement of the U.S. in Kashmir? As of now indications are that India would like to use the U.S. to legitimize its military activities in Kashmir as a war on terror without subjecting itself to any kinds of U.S. pressure on its regional postures.

Until recently the U.S. had imposed sanctions against India and Pakistan for doing things they thought was necessary for their national security and something that the U.S. has already done – develop nuclear weapons. Now that the U.S. needs the two nations for its own security, it is cozying up to them. While these two countries realize that they can use the U.S. for their own purposes, they may not be willing to trust it as yet.

Highly sophisticated Indian and Pakistani lobbies inside the U.S. are more interested in encouraging the U.S. to adopt a partisan role and their influence will also impede the U.S. from acting as an honest broker. These are important barriers to an influential role for the U.S. in the resolution of the Kashmiri crisis.

No Infrastructure for Peace making: In the Middle East crisis there are two important assets for peace making; one, the existence of a foundational principle for peace – land for security and two, the presence of well developed institutional framework for peace making. We know who are the peace negotiators for Israel, for Palestine and for the U.S.. There is no such development in South Asia and peace making will first necessitate the development of tools/frameworks for peace making.

There are two potential principles for peace; The UN resolution demanding a plebiscite in Kashmir that is advocated by Pakistan and rejected by India. The other alternative is the Simla accords of 1972 that India maintains as overarching and Pakistan disagrees. Neither of these two potential principles treats Kashmiris as an independent voice and that could scuttle any resolution between the nuclear powers if Kashmiris themselves are not allowed to represent their own interests.

Two Level Games: Unlike the two main parties in the Middle East conflict, both India and Pakistan are developing democracies. Pakistan is currently going through an undemocratic stage, but nevertheless the presence of well developed political parties and relatively free and widespread media mean that the government cannot take too many decisions without public consent. In the Middle East while Israeli public opinion and the positions of all internal factions is included in the peace process, Palestinians who have a position different from Arafat's are marginalized. The political development of both India and Pakistan makes peace negotiations a two level game. Which means that not only will the two parties have to negotiate terms with each other, they also will have to negotiate their own positions with opposition factions.

In India the Hindu nationalists and in Pakistan Islamic militias will remain a significant challenge to peace making. Thus negotiations will necessarily become two level games – internal negotiations as well as external negotiations. This is definitely an added complexity making the South Asian dispute very difficult to arbitrate.

Kashmiri Diversity: While India and Pakistan often pretend that Kashmiris themselves do not have much voice in this dispute, any final status negotiations will have to incorporate Kashmiri concerns. Unfortunately for all Kashmiris do not speak with a single voice.

First of all there is a displaced Hindu minority, the Pundits, who would like to return to their homes in Jammu and it is safe to assume that unlike the Kashmiri Muslims they have no desire to either become independent or to join Pakistan. Within the Kashmiri Muslims themselves there are pro-India, Pro-Pakistan and pro-independence factions and if Kashmiris are invited to the table, they will have to reach an internal consensus first. That is easily said than done.

If the U.S. genuinely seeks to resolve the Kashmir dispute as part of its overall strategy to eliminate the reasons for terrorism, then in this case the challenge is quite daunting. The U.S. will have to quickly develop a relationship of trust with both India and Pakistan and set things in motion to first build an infrastructure for peace, so that peacemaking can begin in earnest. It will also have to convince both India and Pakistan to allow an open and free dialogue within Kashmir to allow them to arrive at some kind of consensus about their own future so that they will be able to represent themselves effectively.

Pakistan and the Pitfalls of Indo-centric Nationalism

In the fifty-five years since its independence, India has experienced gradual development, frequently marred by conflicts with its neighbors and within the diverse groups it houses, yet all the time managing in miraculous fashion to maintain its democratic credentials. Today without any doubt it is one of the most important emerging global powers after China. Its expanding industrial base, rapidly capitalizing markets, growing competitiveness in cutting-edge technologies, indigenous nuclear and ballistic capability and most importantly its rapidly burgeoning educated and modern middle class, give it the impetus needed to emerge as one of the world's major military as well as economic powers.

Of course not everything in India is "hunky-dory." The growth of fascism coupled with the corrupt body politic which impedes the state from acting decisively against forces that engender hate and factionalism have marginalized the Muslim minority in India, and placed a great strain on the foundations of India's secular democracy. And to make matters worse for Pakistan, India now has the hyper-national BJP firmly in command in New Delhi.

Pakistan on the other hand has very little to crow about. In the fifty-five years of its existence, it has failed to make the important internal structural adjustments necessary for development in the modern environment. Feudalism remains the bane of Pakistan and the strides that it has made towards democracy are unsteady and misguided.

One of the basic advantages of democracy is its leveling effect. Democracy dissipates political power and prevents any one social or ethnic class to monopolize it to advance partisan interests. However in Pakistan, feudal lords straddle even democracy. Political power continues to be in the hands of the landed few and now democracy merely legitimizes the old regime in the eyes of the international community.

Some political scientists refer to such states as quasi-states -- states that enjoy external sovereignty, yet completely lack internal sovereignty. The prevalence of chaos, rioting, corruption and the failure of state institutions to maintain order and writ of law are all indications that the internal control of the state has diminished, making it both unstable and unviable.

Both India and Pakistan are Indo-centric in their orientation although in their tenures as independent states India and Pakistan chose different routes for modernization. While India focused on its five-year plans and became agriculturally independent, then launched a rapid industrialization program, Pakistan exploited its strategic geopolitical location to attract American economic and military aid.

India pursued an Indo-centric domestic policy determined to become one of the developed states through import substitution strategies and extensive development of educational programs. It soon established a healthy industrial base from which it could partake in the global marketplace. More importantly, the emergence of a large educated middle class gave it the base for a civil society that could sustain and develop the fragile democracy it possessed. For commentators in Pakistan it must be a hard pill to swallow, but the fact remains India has concentrated on state building rather than launching jingoistic campaigns against its neighbors.

Pakistan has also pursued Indo-centric stance. But its focus has been on foreign policy. It has defined its goals in terms of India. The overriding concern seems to have been to acquire Kashmir. Other than symbolic and nationalistic significance, Kashmir has done little for either state except to make them fight two wars. Pakistan, rather than focusing on making the initial structural adjustments necessary to provide impetus for the development of a modern state, allowed itself to be dominated by dictators and medieval/feudal power structures. And it remains one of the few states in the world with literacy rates below 40 percent.

The reason why Pakistan has been and continues to be a foreign policy state is because it has no domestic policy and its political elite does not have the will or the need to have one. Domestic policy would require first and foremost the dismantling of pre-independence power structures, the development of a literate modern middle class and taking democratic institutions and democratic transitions of power seriously.

So what has Indo-centric nationalism done for Pakistan? It has placed it in a bipolar situation that is increasingly threatening and expensive both in terms of cost of maintenance and from the perspective of potential consequences.

What, then, must Pakistan do?

To move away from Indo-centric nationalism towards something more focused on state building and development is the obvious answer. How? The answer to that is not simple and must emerge from free and open discussion among all the segments and classes of the Pakistani people. Perhaps the first step would be to defer the Kashmir issue to some kind of "final status discussions" and start by the lowering of trade barriers that have been in place since 1965. This would inevitably lead to economic interdependence.

It is time for the entire nation to do much soul searching and ask itself these questions: Where did we go wrong? Is this why we created Pakistan? Is hating India or coveting Kashmir the only raison d'etre of Pakistan or does it have a more profound vision for its future?

Pakistan: Paradise Lost

Fifty-five years ago, Pakistan the first premeditated Islamic state was born with great hopes and promises; riding on the aspirations, sacrifices and the dedication of millions of Muslims from the Indian subcontinent. The idea behind Pakistan was not only to provide a homeland for Muslims free from the cultural and political domination of Hindus, but also to create an ideological agent that would advance the global interests of Islam and safeguard the lives and faith of Muslims in the region. Pakistan was designed to not only provide a safe haven for Muslims who became a part of Pakistan but also provide security to those unfortunate enough to stay back for various reasons. For the pragmatists behind the quest for a Muslim nation, Pakistan was supposed to be a haven of freedom and opportunity to prosper for Muslims alone. And for the idealists behind this noble idea, Pakistan was envisaged as that city on the hill that would be a beacon not only to the entire *Ummah* but also to the entire humanity; spreading the message of Islam and by example showing Muslims and other nations the straight path.

Today, Pakistan is so far from its intended purpose that, even to a diehard idealist like me, the noble ideas behind its existence seem like the innocent pronouncements of a child; "When I grow up, I wanna be a pilot, or Pele". It has failed on each and every objective that was advanced by its founding fathers as a raison d'etere for Pakistan. Twenty-five years after its formation Pakistanis demonstrated that ethnicity was more important than Islamic solidarity and split into two nations, Pakistan and Bangladesh. The split was bloody and the process violated every relevant principle of Islam. While some may blame India, I believe that India merely exploited an opening offered by the superficial commitment to Islam manifest by the peoples of the two nations.

Pakistan after escaping Hindus and Bengalis is still far from achieving any of its foundational objectives. Its economy is on a steep decline, its democracy is in retreat, its literacy levels still languish in the 20% range, and corruption is at its peak, religious and sectarian fanaticism is at its zenith, political, religious and ethnic violence is the order of the day and men in uniform rule. Nobody, absolutely nobody considers Pakistan as a model nation worthy of emulation for its moral and material progress. Forget the rest of the world, even in the Muslim world Pakistan is not considered as worthy of leadership. In its present condition it can do nothing for Islam or Muslims, and the thousands of Muslims who died for Pakistan must be wondering if their sacrifices were in vain. Pakistan is also not a source of security to the Muslim in the region. Bangladeshis have suffered from its military and Indian Muslims, on a daily basis, suffer the consequences of its unIslamic foreign policy and materialist/nationalistic geopolitics.

But, it is never too late. Pakistan still exists, its security threats are more internal than external and its economic and social challenges are not insurmountable. The nation can still step hard on the brakes and take a U-turn before there is complete collapse of order and Pakistan becomes a failed state like Somalia. But in order that good things may happen, it is time that Pakistani leaders, its political and religious elite and people who shape public opinion at national as well as local levels take stock and make a sincere attempt to return to the fundamental objective of nation building.

A state at the minimum must work for the welfare, security, and economic and moral well being of its citizens. Ideological goals and/or geopolitical ambitions cannot and must not be pursued at the cost of internal order and economic and political stability. For too long Pakistan has sacrificed its internal well being in pursuit of external objectives. Its involvement in Kashmir, Afghanistan and its continued conflict with India have served no other purpose but to bleed Pakistan internally. A nation that could not keep itself intact and has lost half of itself must give up quixotic pursuits of expansionism. Pakistanis must realize that Pakistan and its internal order come first and they must pursue them.

Once the basics have been achieved and stabilized then it can seek to pursue an ideological foreign agenda. Even when it comes to this, I wish Pakistan would seek to establish its Islamic credentials not by engendering armed conflicts but by creating an internal society that would make the world envious of it and seek to emulate it. Moral leadership is the Islamic way and it comes from enlightened living not through the barrel of a Kalashnikov. The Kalashnikov did nothing for the Soviet Union; it will do nothing for Pakistan.

The priorities for Pakistan are clear, at least in my mind. (1) Return to democracy as soon as possible. (2) Disarm civilian population. (3) Identify and prosecute those who purse self-interest through sectarian conflict. (4) Concentrate on education and social development. (5) Strengthen the economy. (6) Begin a serious but peaceful internal dialogue to understand and articulate Pakistan's Islamic mission. It is important for a nation and its people to have a purpose, even better a divine and moral purpose.

What is Pakistan's purpose? Before we can even begin to debate this, there must be peace and prosperity. Morality and ideology have no meaning when the stomach is empty and the heart is full of fear or anger or hate. I hope Pakistanis everywhere will reflect on what each one of them can do, in their own way, to help their nation make its U-turn and fulfill its promise. Yes, kids do grow up to become pilots, and yes Pele's, Jordans, Woods, and Imran Khans are happening all the time.

Egypt: The Core of Arab Intellect

In more ways than one, Egypt is the heart and the mind of the Arab world. Discourses, both secular as well as Islamic, emerging from Egypt have shaped the frames of references employed by Arabs everywhere. Several streams of ideas such as Islamic liberalism as manifest by the ideas of Khalid M. Khalid, Islamic modernism a la Muhammad Abduh and Rashid Rida, Islamism as in Hassan Al Banna and Syed Qutb and Islamic moderation as in the works of Muhammad al Ghazali, have all originated in Egypt. Islamic Marxism as in the works of Hassan Hanafi has also found a place in the voices of Egypt. Egyptian thinkers too have dominated secular Arab voices. Contemporary Arab culture has also been shaped to a great extent by Egyptian cinema that has been popular in the entire Arab world for over a half century.

Politically too, Egypt is the center of Arab consciousness. If the Arab world has to take any important step, Egypt must lead. Without

Egyptian leadership the Arab world would be rudderless. There has been no Arab-Israeli war since Egypt made peace with Israel. The fact that Washington continues to invest nearly 2 Billion dollars every year as a renewal fees for Egyptian cooperation in the region is indicative of Egypt's geopolitical importance.

Therefore in order to understand the present and the future of the Arab world, it is important to watch the Egyptian pulse.

In the last fifty years two powerful and antithetical ideas emerged from Egypt that continue to shape the internal dynamics of the Arab world. These ideas/movements are Arab socialism and Muslim brotherhood. While the first idea gained popularity as a surrogate to the popularity of Jamal Abdel-Nasser, the second gained momentum after the execution of Syed Qutb. These two trends are the backbones of Arab politics today, with Arab socialism embedded in the state machinery and Islamic resurgence taking a strong foothold in the civil society.

From an Islamic perspective, the presence of Al Azhar University in Egypt adds to the influence that Egypt exercises over the Islamic consciousness of the Arab world.   Egypt's strengths are Arab strengths and similarly Egypt's weaknesses are Arab weaknesses.

The absence of democracy and the continuation of authoritarian regimes in Egypt undermine the prospects for democratization in the entire Arab world. Similarly the Egyptian method of containment of Islam by state apparatus through repression as well as cooption is replicated in the rest of the Arab world.   If there must be change in the socio-political context of the Arab world then that change must begin in Egyptian society. It is not for nothing that the U.S. subsidizes the Egyptian state machinery's capacity to keep a tight control on the trends within Egypt.

The Palestinian cause has literally been surrendered by the Arab world since the famous Camp David accord between Egypt and Israel. Today Egypt plays the role of the moderator. Every time there is anger and Arab states determine to take some punitive action against Israel, Egyptian leadership call for a summit and advocate a moderate response. In essence Egypt has kept the responses to Israeli atrocities by Arab states within acceptable limits.   In effect making

Egyptian foreign policy, Arab foreign policy.

The Islamic movement in America too is strongly influenced by Egypt. Many prominent American Muslim organizations have been created and are still managed by individuals with strong ties to the *Ikhwan Al-Muslimeen* (Muslim Brotherhood). One of the earliest books published by American Trust Publications was the English translation of Syed Qutb's *Milestones* and one of the issues of the *Islamic Horizons* was a special issue dedicated to Hassan Al Banna. Azhari scholars continue to enjoy great respect and hold several jobs as Imams in American Mosques. As Imams they control the Friday sermons and through these sermons the interpretation of Islam in America.

Egypt is at once both stagnant as well as a vibrant society. It has managed to remain intellectually alive without fully transforming itself and has continued to remain backward and underdeveloped without fully losing the vitality of its soul. Egypt is like Islam in Egypt. It is there, not in control but not completely subdued, either.

Slowly Muslim intellectuals in Egypt are realizing that neither Arab socialism nor Islamic revivalism has succeeded in addressing the many problems of Egypt and the Arab world. There is at least an emerging consensus in Egypt that whatever the future of Egypt, Islam will play a central role. What is not clear is what that role will be and who, the state Ulema, or the traditional scholars or the Muslim Brotherhood, will provide the dominant interpretation of Islam. Until these questions are settled, "Which Islam" and "How Islam", Egyptian society will not stabilize, and neither will the Arab world.

Iraq: Between Power and Pain

The modern Iraq was clearly the most advanced and developed of Arab societies. It matched Egypt in political and intellectual matters and with the additional help of oil resources, Iraq outstripped Egypt in matters of modernization and human resources development.

The transformation of Iraq from a prosperous, thriving and healthy society to a starving, devastated and pathetic dump is one of the most tragic tales of the twentieth century. The story of Iraq is also illustrative of the decadent and unenlightened politics of the Arab World in particular and the Muslim World in general.

The contemporary history of Iraq can be divided into three stages. The first stage was the chaotic development of a nation-state, driven primarily by geopolitical intrigue between global powers. The second stage marks the two decades of oil driven rapid development. And the two decades of gradual devastation as a result of two wars, each of which has lasted nearly a decade, marks the third and present stage.

During the sixties and seventies, Iraq made rapid strides. The oil crisis of 1973 had quadrupled oil revenues and the surplus was used to finance industrial and infrastructure development. Hundred of thousands of Iraqis went overseas to the U.S. and Europe on government scholarships and came home with advanced degrees in science and technology. Universities thrived, new business were launched and once again, Mesopotamia the cradle of civilization, began to prosper.

However in 1979, Saddam Hussein became president and Iraq has since seen nothing but a downward spiral. Saddam inherited an advanced nation with a modern army and enormous financial resources. It is difficult to guess whether the geopolitical decisions he made were a result of miscalculation or a megalomaniacal mentality that refuses to see reason. Whatever the causes, he made two big mistakes, one in 1980 and one in 1990 and both have caused Iraq untold damage.

In 1980 Saddam invaded Iran and began an 8-year war between Muslim nations that caused a cumulative damage of over U.S. $550 billion USD and took one million Muslim lives. Eventually the Iran-Iraq war came to an end in 1988 with no gain or loss to either of the two countries. Iraq had two reasons for initiating the war against Iran. In 1980 Iran was under great turmoil as the Islamic revolution was beginning to consolidate itself. Saddam may have thought that this was an opportune moment to start a quick war and annex some of Iran's oil rich areas. The initial gains made by Iraq justify this line of thinking. But what he had not factored in was the spirit of the Iranian people. They threw everything they had including their children at him and made Iraq pay heavily for this misadventure.

Iran unfortunately was weakened considerably by this war, espe-cially at the time when its Islamic revolution needed all its resources to withstand the economic war being waged against it by the U.S..

Saddam also feared that the call for internationalizing the Islamic revolution made by Imam Khomeini might be answered by the Iraqi Shii who are in majority in Iraq. Perhaps he calculated that the best way to preempt the spread of the Iranian revolution would be to attack it.

Within two years after the war with Iran, Saddam got into a dis-pute with another neighbor; this time Kuwait. Believing that the U.S. would not intervene if he invaded Kuwait, Saddam invaded and annexed Kuwait in August of 1990. This single act has cast the spell of doom on Iraq. The U.S. led a 128-nation coalition, which included nearly all Muslims countries in a war against Iraq. The war cost near-ly U.S. $200 billion USD, of which Saudi Arabia and the royal family of Kuwait spent nearly U.S. $165 billion.

It is important that Muslims everywhere remember that the major part of the funding for the destruction of Iraq came from fellow Arab/Muslim nations. Iran interestingly remained neutral in this war.

The war and the subsequent sanctions (slow motion war) have systematically reduced a once prosperous, advanced, industrialized and sophisticated society into rubble. Today people, especially chil-dren are dying of malnutrition, epidemics and lack of food. Even though the sanctions regime is loosing its cohesiveness there seems to be no immediate relief forthcoming for the beleaguered people of Iraq.

The consciousness about the suffering of the people of Iraq has been on the rise and more and more people are campaigning against them. While Muslims in general are aware of what has happened to the Iraqi people, there is a need to put things in perspective.

The general feeling among Muslims is that the saga of Iraq is just another instance of the West's unending campaign against Islam. Some Muslims, who have a slightly better understanding of Iraq's his-tory, argue that Saddam is essentially an American agent sent to destroy Iraq. Some others, blessed with a more powerful imagination, manage to find a Zionist connection behind Saddam.

All these theories are designed to blame the West for the misery and the evil in the Muslim world and to portray Muslims as innocent victims. I believe that all these conspiracy theories are a reflection of the simplistic models that inform popular Muslim thought. These theories are also a means to look away from the disturbing truth that there is indeed something deeply rotten in the Arab world.

Let us dismantle each of the above-mentioned conspiracy theories one after the other. Yes indeed, Saddam Hussein is a cruel leader, who does not care for the suffering of his people and is motivated only by desires of grandeur and glory for himself. A quick survey of the Arab world will show that he is not alone. In fact most of the Arab world, is ruled by such inhumane, authoritarian and self-serving leaders whose sole purpose is to prolong their rule for as long as possible.

Saddam Hussein is not an exception but the norm. He reflects the present ethos of the region, which is dominated by an authoritarian streak that has no respect for the rights, and dignity of the weak and the underprivileged. The condition of expatriate workers, women, religious minorities and the manner in which they are systematically abused and exploited by the culture as well as the states of the region is indicative. Abuse of power and lack of civility is a way of life. Every man is a despot in himself. Whatever their sphere of influence, from family, to business, to bureaucracy to the state, the Arab wishes to dictate. It is no accident that democracy has taken root in nearly all regions of the world except in the Arab world. It is also in the Arab world that one still finds the presence of real monarchs who exercise excessive control over their subjects. Saddam Hussein is not alien to this culture. He is merely representative of excess in the current maladies of the region.

During the Iran-Iraq war most of the Arab nations supported Saddam Hussein, morally, politically and financially. No one cared for the utter misery he brought first upon the Iranian people and then on his own people. He was hailed as the great hero who stood up to the Shii nation. Muslims did not take out processions or lament the lost of one million Muslim lives that were lost in that war. In his war against Iran, Saddam was an Arab-Sunni agent, not a Western or Zionist agent. The fact that he weakened both Iran and Iraq, much to the delight of Israel and the U.S., does not mean that he represents their interests. These interests coincided with the interests of the Gulf nations and so he was hailed as an Arab hero.

During the Gulf War, Many Muslims admired Saddam. He was hailed as the new Saladin. Some Muslims looked forward to the mother of all battles. Their mouths watered at the prospects of seeing American blood flow in the deserts of Arabia. Saddam suddenly became the embodiment of *jihad* and there was no talk of his being an American or a Zionist agent. The same people who condemn him today, hailed him then. If Iraq had become another Vietnam, then Saddam would forever have become a great Muslim/Arab hero. But in his defeat he also lost the support of Arabs and Muslims. The new Saladin suddenly became a Western agent.

Even until today, Muslims have not condemned Saddam for using chemical weapons against Kurds (who are also Muslim) and Iran.

On the subject of sanctions Muslims condemn the U.S. and have conducted several protest marches in New York and Washington. Muslims must realize that these sanctions are still sought by Muslim nations like Saudi Arabia and Kuwait. Saddam is not a U.S. agent, it is the U.S. which is a Saudi-Kuwait agent destroying an Arab nation to protect other Arab nations from it. These sanctions cannot work without the complete cooperation of Muslim nations bordering Iraq.

Muslims all over the world, who were with Saddam when he invaded Iran and stood up to the U.S., are as much agents of the West as Saddam is. They supported him knowing fully well that he has the blood of over a million Muslims on his hands.

The misery and the suffering of the Iraqis, the Arabs and all the Muslims will continue even after Saddam. For as long as authoritarianism is encouraged in Muslim cultures it will continue to produce dictators.

When as a culture we do not respect human rights, individual dignity and democracy, we only abuse ourselves. The culture of despotism in the Arab and Muslim world has brought pain, indignity and suffering to Muslims and not to anybody else. Someday we will realize that, and as families, as groups, as communities and nations, we will imbibe the virtues of *shura* and mutual respect.